# Workbook

## First Certificate

# Direct

*Mary Spratt*
*Bob Obee*

**CAMBRIDGE**
UNIVERSITY PRESS

PUBLISHED BY THE PRESS SYNDICATE OF THE UNIVERSITY OF CAMBRIDGE
The Pitt Building, Trumpington Street, Cambridge, United Kingdom

CAMBRIDGE UNIVERSITY PRESS
The Edinburgh Building, Cambridge CB2 2RU, UK
40 West 20th Street, New York, NY 10011–4211, USA
10 Stamford Road, Oakleigh, VIC 3166, Australia
Ruiz de Alarcón 13, 28014 Madrid, Spain
Dock House, The Waterfront, Cape Town 8001, South Africa

http://www.cambridge.org

First published 2001

Printed in the United Kingdom at the University Press, Cambridge
Designed and produced by Pentacor plc, UK

*Typeface* Bliss 10.5pt on 13pt leading
*System* QuarkXPress®

ISBN 0 521 65416 5 Student's Book
ISBN 0 521 65415 7 Teacher's Book
ISBN 0 521 65413 0 Class Cassette Set
ISBN 0 521 65414 9 Workbook
ISBN 0 521 79939 2 Workbook With Answers

# Contents

# Thanks

We would both like to thank Alison Silver and Charlotte Adams for all the help and support they have given during the planning and editing stages of the production of this course. Their patience and attention to detail were impressive.

Bob Obee would also like to thank Maureen, Florence Popsy and Nellie Louise for their care, guidance and support. And Mary would like to thank Tim for his humorous forbearance.

# Acknowledgements

Cover design by Pentacor plc, High Wycombe.
Text design and page make up by Pentacor plc, High Wycombe.

The authors and publishers would like to thank the teachers and students who trialled and commented on the material:

Argentina: Mariel Latis, Liliana Luna; Brazil: Chris Dupont; France: Harry Crawford; Greece: Christine Barton, Gaynor Williams; Poland: Tadeusz Wolanski; Spain: Mark Appleby, Henny Burke, Samantha Lewis; UK: Jane Hann, Roger Scott.

Thanks also to Diane Jones (picture research), Sophie Dukan (permissions research) and Ruth Carim (proof-reading).

The authors and publishers are grateful to the following for permission to reproduce copyright material. It has not been possible to identify the sources of all the material used and in such cases the publishers would welcome information from copyright owners.

Texts on pp. 8 and 29: from *Strange but True* by Tim Healey; Octopus Books; pp. 13 and 82: Marie Claire 1998 © IPC Magazines; p. 90: High Life © Premier Media Partners; pp. 16 (by Rose Ong), 42 (by Clifford Lo) and 52: reprinted with permission from SCMP.com Limited; pp. 17 and 88: © Agence France-Presse; pp. 20-1 (by Alex O'Connell), 26, 30, 35, 77 (by Ben Macintyre), 78 (by Dom Foulsham): © The Times Newspapers; p. 23: by Barbara Leigh-Evans, Leisure Publications 1997; pp. 24 and 47: from *Eye Witness Travel Guide to Italy*, Dorling Kindersley 1999; pp. 32 and 80: extracted from *The Lost Continent* by Bill Bryson, published by Black Swan, a division of Transworld Publishers. All rights reserved; dictionary entries on pp. 32 and 57: from *The Cambridge International Dictionary of English*; quotes on p. 34: from *The Penguin Dictionary of Modern Humorous Quotations* by Fred Metcalf, Penguin 1987; p. 41: © Sha Tin College; pp. 44 and 75-6: from *The Guinness Book of Oddities* by Geoff Tibballs © Geoff Tibballs 1995; pp. 46 and 48: Reader's Digest (June 1998); p. 47: by Jerry Shriver, USA Today; pp. 51–2: by Vivien Donald from *Offbeat Careers: 60 Ways to Avoid Becoming an Accountant*, Kogan Page 1987; p. 58: Star Tribune 1998; p. 60: from *Essential Thailand* by Christine Osborne © Automobile Association Developments Ltd (1990) LIC026/01; p. 68: courtesy of Focus Magazine © National Magazine Company; p. 72 from *The Rough Guide to England*, published January 2000 by Rough Guides Ltd; p. 73: by Albino Ochero-Okello from London: The Lives of the City © Albino Ochero-Okello; p. 77: Cosmopolitan 1998; p. 78 from *Colemanballs* edited by Barry Fantoni, Private Eye 1982; p. 81: BBC Online 1999; p. 83: National Geographic 1996; p. 86: by Steve James, Reuters 1998; p. 87: Associated Press 1998; p. 88: Guardian Weekly 1999; pp. 92–96: © UCLES.

We are grateful to the following for permission to reproduce copyright photographs:

Photographs on p. 8: Hulton Getty; p. 12 (top): Telegraph Colour Library/Mel Yates; p. 12 (bottom): Rex Features/Eva; p.13: Camera Press; pp.18, 30, 66: Gareth Boden; p. 20: Camera Press/Gianni Murature; p. 23: Telegraph Colour Library/Rob Jewell; p. 32: Pictures Colour Library; p. 36 (photo 1): Powerstock Zefa/Charles Tyler, (photo 2): Stone/John Lamb, (photo 3): Pictures Colour Library, (photo 4): Stone/Chris Harvey; (photo 5): Camera Press/Richard Open, (photo 6): Telegraph Colour Library/B & M Productions, (photo 8): Stone/Cosmo Candina; p. 42 (left): Stone/David Young Wolff; p. 42 (right): Stone/Dennis O'Clair; p. 44: Oxford Scientific Films/Hall and Ball Archive; p. 45: Rex Features/Geoff Wilkinson; p. 46: Stone/David Job; p. 48: Stone/Mike Magnuson; p. 62: Rex Features; p. 67 (top left and bottom left): Pictorial Press; p. 67 (top right): Stone/Ron Sherman; p. 67 (bottom right): Rex Features/F. Castell; p. 70: Camera Press/Illustrated London News; p. 71: Collins/Gareth Boden; p. 72 (top): Stone/David Kreiger; p. 72 (bottom): Stone/Jean-François Gate; p. 74: Pictorial Press; p. 78: Popperfoto; p. 83: Stone/Glen Allison; p. 84 (top): Stone/Michael Rosenfield; p. 84 (bottom): Camera Press/Flash Bang Wallop; p. 90 (top left): Powerstock Zefa/John Conrad, (top middle): Stone/Art Wolfe, (top right): Stone/Keren Su, (bottom left): Rex Features/Dave Hartley, (bottom middle): BBC Natural History Unit/Tom Walmsley, (bottom right): BBC Natural History Unit/Lockwood & Dattatri.

Illustrations by: Phillip Burrows, Kate Charlesworth, Simon Turner, Kath Walker, Ian West.

# Introduction for students

## What is the aim of the
## *First Certificate Direct* Workbook?

This Workbook aims to give you extra opportunities to practise your English, and revise and consolidate the things you have learnt in the Student's Book of *First Certificate Direct*. It will help you develop your general English, the English you need for the FCE exam and your exam techniques.

The Workbook also aims to provide you with materials that you can easily work with outside class – by yourself or with friends. This allows you to work at your own pace, and to choose to concentrate on those things you feel you most need.

## What does the
## *First Certificate Direct* Workbook contain?

- The Workbook contains 14 units, which cover the same topics as the units in the Student's Book, looked at from different points of view – so you meet new language and new themes.

- Each unit has these six sections:
  **Reading**
  **Writing**
  **Grammar**
  **Vocabulary**
  **Preparation for speaking**
  **Exam focus**

- The sections develop the language, the language skills and the exam skills practised in the same unit of the Student's Book.

- 'Dealing with the FCE exam' (see page 92) includes an overview of the exam, information on the content and marking of each paper, and useful tips for how to approach each part of the exam.

# What is the best way to use the *First Certificate Direct* Workbook?

- The activities in the Workbook are designed so that you can do them outside class – by yourself or with friends.

- Your teacher may ask you to do some of the Workbook activities in or outside class. You could also choose activities yourself to work on outside class, selecting those activities you feel you need to work on most. Use the Map of the book in the Student's Book and the Section list opposite to help you make your choices.

- As the topics and activities in the Workbook follow those in the same unit of the Student's Book, it is a good idea to do the Workbook activities **after** you have done the corresponding work in the Student's Book.

- **exam task** You will see that many of the Workbook activities are exam tasks. This is to give you extra practice for the exam and to build up your confidence in handling exam tasks. They have the same symbol as the Student's Book.

- The 'Preparation for speaking' sections give you activities to carry out that will help you to improve your speaking. They ask you to plan and think about what you would say, for example, or choose suitable language, or practise your pronunciation. These are a very useful way of improving your speaking by yourself.

- When you use the Workbook, make sure you use a good dictionary too. We suggest: *Cambridge International Dictionary of English*, *Cambridge International Dictionary of English CD-ROM*, or *Cambridge Dictionaries Online*: www.http://dictionary.cambridge.org

- You could also refer to a good grammar reference book. We suggest: *English Grammar in Use* by Raymond Murphy, published by Cambridge University Press.

- Keep notes in a file. Organise your file into different sections, e.g. Grammar, Vocabulary. In the grammar section you could note down any new or interesting grammatical structures you come across. In the vocabulary section, you could write down a list of new words and expressions and their meanings. You could then test yourself or your friends from time to time, to see if you remember the words and their meanings. You can also play games with the words, e.g. word bingo or associations.

- Some students prefer working by themselves while others like to work with a friend. Decide which is best for you when using this Workbook.

We hope you enjoy working with the *First Certificate Direct* Workbook and find it useful for your studies. Good luck with your English, with your studies and with the exam!

*Mary Spratt*

# People

*Sergeant Shoichi Yokoi*

## Reading

**1** You are going to read a story about a Japanese soldier who survived in the jungle on the island of Guam for years after the end of the second world war. In this true story many different words are used to talk about the emotions of this soldier. Can you predict which of the following will be mentioned in connection with:

a   his time in hiding?

b   his eventual return to Japan?

> faithful   disbelief   fear
> shocked   discipline   loyalty
> ashamed   puzzled

Then as you read the text, see how accurate your predictions were.

**2** **exam task** Read the text again. Seven sentences have been removed from it. Choose from the sentences **A–H** the one which fits each gap (1–6). There is one extra sentence which you do not need to use. There is an example at the beginning (0).

## Japan's Last Wartime Survivor

On 26th January 1972, The Times reported: 'A Japanese soldier who remained faithful to his orders never to surrender was captured on Guam yesterday after 28 years of hiding.' **0** **H** He was wearing trousers and a jacket made from tree and bark fibre. **1**

For 28 years, Yokoi had lived in a time warp. He had never heard either of the atomic bomb or of television and stared in disbelief when told that a jet aircraft could return him to his home town of Nagoya in three hours. He knew that on Guam, at least, the war was over because of leaflets he had found scattered through the jungle. **2** Yokoi had held out, fearing he might be executed if he surrendered.

Japan was haunted by Yokoi's experience, which echoed largely forgotten values of samurai loyalty and discipline. In one tragic incident four young Japanese boys were killed when trying to build a tunnelled cave like Yokoi's on Guam. And if Japan was haunted by Yokoi's experience so was the survivor himself. **3** They were punishing him, he believed, for planning to return to Japan alone.

Guam itself had now become a popular resort for Japanese tourists. When he saw honeymooning couples, boys with long hair and girls with short skirts, he was shocked and asked reporters 'Are these really Japanese?'. **4** 'You are different Japanese,' he told them. 'There must be other Japanese people.'

Yokoi's return was a nationally televised event, which aroused intense curiosity. About 5,000 people gathered at the airport. **5** One, dressed in his former uniform, held up a banner declaring: 'Only Mr Yokoi still possesses the Spirit of Japan.' An official reception, headed by the Welfare Minister, was there to meet him as he emerged unsteadily from the plane.

At a crowded press conference held later, Yokoi looked tired and drawn but surprisingly fit. Questions had been carefully prepared by Japanese journalists, inviting the former soldier to express joy on returning and to make suitably appropriate comments about the horrors of war. **6** He was ashamed to come back, he said, and his sole purpose was to make a full report on what happened in Guam as this might be useful if Japan had to fight another war.

---

**A** But of the larger dimension, he was quite ignorant.

**B** Yokoi made no secret of the fact that he was looking forward to settling back into life at home.

**C** He had been a tailor when conscripted in 1941 and used a pair of scissors he had had throughout the war to shape his clothes and cut his hair.

**D** Among them were many veterans of the old Imperial Army.

**E** In the Guam hospital where he was being cared for, he suffered nightmares about the spirits of departed comrades.

**F** To their embarrassment, Yokoi appeared not to share the expected sentiments.

**G** The reporters themselves were just as puzzling and foreign to him.

**H** Sergeant Shoichi Yokoi, then 56, was heavily bearded when found.

**3** Which of these details do you find most surprising about Yokoi's story? Why?

- He had known the war was over in Guam.
- He knew nothing about modern Guam.
- He felt ashamed to be returning home.
- Many people thought of him as a hero.

**4** The text contains many words about people's feelings and emotions. Complete this table.

| Adjective | Noun | Adjective | Noun |
|---|---|---|---|
| embarrassed | embarrassment | loyal | |
| faithful | | | discipline |
| | fear | ashamed | |
| shocked | | curious | |
| | joy | popular | |

## Writing

**1** Look at the first halves of these three letters. What types of letter are they? Choose one of the words from the list.

enquiry    request    application    apology
complaint    acceptance    confirmation    refusal

**A**

Dear Sir/Madam,

Having seen your advertisement in the Echo of Tuesday March 5th, I would like further information about the fishing trips you organise. I am a keen amateur and go fishing whenever I can but I have never been on an organised trip. I would be particularly interested in trips to the Yorkshire area.

**B**

Dear Sir/Madam,
I am writing in connection with an incident which took place on Tuesday March 19th. I imagine other people may have written to you about this matter as well. Last Tuesday as I was walking down Mill Street at about 4 pm, I saw a security guard come out of the side exit of your store. He started shouting at a homeless man who was sitting in the doorway and then kicked him and threw the hot coffee he was holding in his face.

**C**

Dear Sir/Madam,

I am writing in connection with your advertisement for someone to work as a part-time baby-sitter. I am 16 years old and at present studying for my 'A' level exams. I have a younger sister who I sometimes look after while my parents are out so I am used to being around small children.

**2** Think about what the writer of these letters wants in each case. Which writer:

1  will ask for a leaflet/form (further details)? ☐

2  will recommend what the reader of the letter should do? ☐

3  will talk about when he or she is available? ☐

4  will ask questions about payment? ☐ ☐

5  will try to show they understand the reader's position? ☐

6  might begin the next paragraph: 'Such behaviour is ...'? ☐

7  will ask what they might have to bring? ☐

8  might use the words: 'I'd be happy to call round ...'? ☐

**3** Now finish each letter with one or two short paragraphs using the points in **2** as a guide.

## Grammar

**1** Imagine that the second speaker in each of these dialogues disagrees with what the first speaker says. Use one of the modal verbs below to show this. Complete each response as shown in the example.

> mustn't   must   can   can't   have to
> don't have to   might   should

1 **A:** He won't be there yet.
   **B:** Oh, I think he ......*should be*.......

2 **A:** I think you're supposed to be over 18.
   **B:** No, you ........................ be.

3 **A:** I don't think she likes me.
   **B:** You ........................ take it personally.

4 **A:** I'm sure he's living somewhere else.
   **B:** He ........................ be. I called him yesterday.

5 **A:** She should win easily.
   **B:** You never know, she ........................ not.

6 **A:** I don't think you're required to show your ID.
   **B:** Oh, yes, you ........................ or you can't get in.

7 **A:** She's probably not going now.
   **B:** Oh, come on, she ........................ be. It's important.

8 **A:** I don't think he's ever very busy.
   **B:** Oh, he ........................ be sometimes.

**2** Look at these key words. Imagine these are the key words that you will need to use to complete each sentence in **3**. Match one of these words to each sentence in **3** as in the example. Doing this first should help you think about the exact meaning of the first sentence.

> had better   should   supposed   expected
> allowed   might not   can't   may

**3** For questions 1–8, complete the second sentence so that it has a similar meaning to the first sentence, using the word given (which you chose in **2**). Do not change the word given. You must use between two and five words, including the word given.

1 They might let us attend the ceremony after all.
   EXAMPLE: *allowed*
   We ...*might be allowed to go*... to the ceremony after all.

2 We ought to take something like a box of chocolates.
   We ........................ something like a box of chocolates.

3 It's possible that people won't turn up if the weather is this bad.
   People ........................ if the weather is this bad.

4 I think you have to wear trousers and long sleeves if you want to go in.
   I think you ........................ trousers and long sleeves if you want to go in.

5 You'll have to get up and take part in the dancing.
   You'll be ........................ and take part in the dancing.

6 I'm sure that isn't an original costume – it looks too new.
   That ........................ an original costume – it looks too new.

7 I expect they'll be here soon – it's almost eight.
   They ........................ here soon – it's almost eight.

8 It's possible that they will ask you to make a speech.
   You ........................ to make a speech.

# Vocabulary

**1** exam task For questions 1–15, read the text below and decide which answer A, B, C or D best fits each space. There is an example at the beginning (0).

## SEASONAL ADVICE

If you are about to graduate from school or college this summer and feel (0) ..B.. need of a little advice about what's important (1) ..... life, you could do a lot worse than consider the words of (2) ..... that were read out on my last day at school:

Do not expect to understand the value of your youth until it has (3) ...... . But you can be sure that thirty years from now you'll (4) ..... back on life and (5) .....  just how good things were.

Try not to worry (6) ..... the future – or at least be aware that worrying never really helps to (7) ..... anything. Real troubles will always sneak up and (8) ..... you by surprise. But remember it doesn't do any harm to do something that (9) ..... you every so often.

Do not lie and cheat – especially in love – and  do not (10) ..... up with people who deceive you. Do not let opportunities pass you by, as the time to do things simply runs (11) ..... . Today is almost certainly more important than tomorrow.

It helps to be kind (12) ..... neighbours and colleagues – it's nice to know they'll (13) ..... you when you're not around. Friends come and go, but there are a precious (14) ..... that you should try and (15) ..... on to. Without quality friends, quality time is harder to come by.

| 0 | A | on | B | in | C | to | D | so |
|---|---|---|---|---|---|---|---|---|
| 1 | A | at | B | with | C | in | D | of |
| 2 | A | knowledge | B | learning | C | opinion | D | wisdom |
| 3 | A | gone | B | been | C | lasted | D | spent |
| 4 | A | come | B | look | C | think | D | go |
| 5 | A | remind | B | rethink | C | recall | D | reappear |
| 6 | A | for | B | at | C | about | D | on |
| 7 | A | triumph | B | succeed | C | solve | D | deal |
| 8 | A | get | B | happen | C | appear | D | take |
| 9 | A | dislikes | B | scares | C | fears | D | minds |
| 10 | A | look | B | come | C | put | D | bring |
| 11 | A | out | B | down | C | off | D | over |
| 12 | A | about | B | to | C | for | D | in |
| 13 | A | remark | B | care | C | wish | D | miss |
| 14 | A | some | B | little | C | several | D | few |
| 15 | A | take | B | hold | C | stay | D | stick |

**2** 📖 exam task For questions 1–10, read the text below. Use the word given in capitals at the end of each line to form a word that fits in the space in the same line. There is an example at the beginning (0).

TWINS

The love-hate **(0)** *connection* between twins is very      **CONNECT**
well documented. **(1)** ..... , rivalry and fighting are      **COMPETE**
an **(2)** ..... of the need for attention. If one      **EXPRESS**
marries and the other doesn't, or one **(3)** .....      **SUCCESS**
materially and the other doesn't, this can create
intense **(4)** ..... . So twins should be      **DIFFICULT**
encouraged to develop individual **(5)** ..... , tastes      **FRIEND**
and **(6)** ..... . For some twins, finding a partner is      **LIFE**
especially tough as no one ever measures up to their
**(7)** ..... partner – their twin. Also, if a non-twin      **ORIGIN**
marries a twin, they have to understand that there
is already an extremely close **(8)** ..... to rival their      **RELATION**
**(9)** ..... . And apart from the psychology, bringing up twins      **MARRY**
is challenging on physical, **(10)** ..... and practical levels.      **FINANCE**

# Preparation for speaking

**1** Look at the common expressions below (**a–p**). What is the speaker doing in each case? Match the expressions to one of these functions:

1 making excuses ........ ........

2 refusing ........ ........

3 offering encouragement ........ ........

4 offering help ........ ........

5 warning/threatening ........ ........

6 congratulating ........ ........

7 seeking information ........ ........

8 accepting ........ ........

**2** Bring a newspaper or magazine story to class about someone that impressed you. Prepare to tell other members of the class about:
- their character
- what they have done
- what most impressed you

---

**a** You'd better not.

**b** No way.

**c** I've got too much on.

**d** *I'm dying to know.*

**e** Can I give you a hand with that?

**f** Thanks, I'd appreciate it.

**g** *I promise I won't tell.*

**h** I'd rather not, if that's OK.

**i** *Cheer up, things could be worse.*

**j** That's very nice of you.

**k** It's no more than you deserve.

**l** You'll be fine.

**m** *Is there anything I can do?*

**n** I'm really pleased for you.

**o** I wouldn't if I were you.

**p** *I can't make it, I'm afraid.*

# Exam focus Paper 1 Reading

## Part 2 Multiple choice

There are two different types of question in the exam task below. Questions 1–5 relate to specific parts of the text. First, identify the part of the text which contains the specific information. Then try to eliminate the three wrong answers before choosing the correct alternative. Question 6 requires you to think about information in different parts of the text. Read through the three opening paragraphs again before selecting your answer.

**exam task** Read the text below about a famous American singer. For questions 1–6, choose the answer (A, B, C or D) which you think fits best according to the text

### Tammy Wynette
#### The Heroine of Heartbreak

Tammy Wynette fulfilled many a girl's fantasy from the American South by moving from the cotton fields to become America's self-styled First Lady of Country Music. Along the way, she sold more records than any other female country-and-western star. But as well as 35 number one hits and White House performances for four different presidents, the so-called 'Heroine of Heartbreak' also had five husbands and four children, seventeen surgical operations and once experienced a kidnapping.

Her life story, she freely admitted, was 'ridiculous – mostly because I've made it that way'. The best thing that perhaps could be said about Wynette's personal dramas was that they provided an endless source of good material. 'I write better when I'm depressed,' she claimed, and was once accused of setting to music 'every angry word and flying plate'.

As with everything else throughout Tammy's career, her beginnings in music were closely connected to a personal tragedy. Her father who'd dreamed of becoming a professional musician himself, was very ill when Tammy was born and he died when she was just nine months old. On his death bed, he made his wife promise to encourage their daughter to take an interest in music, if she showed any talent. Young Wynette, as she became known, began taking piano lessons at the age of eight, and she became so good at playing by ear that her piano teacher eventually gave up on her.

Tammy only really started to take her singing ambitions seriously, however, after the break-up of her first marriage to Euple Byrd. Now with three children and after several frustrating and fruitless trips to Nashville in search of a recording contract, she was persuaded that she would have a better chance if she moved there and so it was in 1966 that she packed her children and their few belongings into her car and drove to 'Music City'. Euple happened to drive past just as she was leaving. 'In your dreams, baby, in your dreams,' he said when she told him her plans. (Years later, when Euple asked her to sign a photograph, Tammy was able to return this sentiment in writing.) 67

Arriving in Nashville, Tammy would leave the children in the car while she did the rounds of the record companies. She eventually slipped past an absent secretary and into the offices of producer Billy Sherrill at Epic Records. He remembers her as a pale, desperate-looking girl but he instantly fell for her voice with what he called its 'teardrop quality'. And the rest, as they say, is history…

1 The opening paragraph suggests
   A Tammy's career was a short one.
   B Tammy kidnapped someone.
   C Tammy enjoyed good health.
   D Tammy grew up in a farming area.

2 In response to questions about her difficulties, Tammy
   A pointed to her success.
   B blamed herself.
   C called the questions 'ridiculous'.
   D refused to answer.

3 Tammy's songs
   A were written for plays.
   B were criticised for the music.
   C were based on her experience.
   D were written by a friend.

4 Tammy moved to Nashville because
   A previous trips had been encouraging.
   B her ex-husband encouraged her to go.
   C becoming a singer might be easier there.
   D she could easily afford to.

5 'This' in line 67 refers to
   A the photograph.
   B her dreams.
   C Euple's request for a signature.
   D Euple's comment on her plans.

6 The writer suggests that
   A Tammy kept her personal life and music separate.
   B Tammy relied too much on other people.
   C Tammy's personal life limited her success.
   D Tammy succeeded despite many difficulties.

# 2 Health matters

## Reading

**1** Do you know what the 'body clock' is? How does it work? What does it do? Read this article to find the answers.

### THE BODY CLOCK

Why is it that flying to New York from London will leave you feeling less tired than flying to London from New York? The answer may be a clear case of biology not being able to keep up with technology.

Deep inside the brain there is a 'clock' that governs every aspect of the body's functioning: sleep and wake cycles, levels of alertness, performance, mood, hormone levels, digestion, body temperature and so on. It regulates all of these functions on a 24-hour basis and is called the circadian clock (from the Latin, *circa* 'about' + *dies* 'day').

This body clock programmes us to be sleepy twice a day, between 3-5 am and again between 3-5 pm. Afternoon tea and siesta times are all cultural responses to our natural biological sleepiness in the afternoon.

One of the major causes of the travellers' malady known as jet lag is the non-alignment of a person's internal body clock with clocks in the external world.

Crossing different time zones confuses the circadian clock, which then has to adjust to the new time and patterns of light and activity. To make matters more complex, not all internal body functions adjust at the same rate. So your sleep/wake may adjust to a new time zone at one rate, while your temperature adjusts at a different pace. Your digestion may be on a different schedule altogether.

Though we live in a 24-hour day, the natural tendency of the body clock is to extend our day beyond 24 hours. It is contrary to our biological programming to 'shrink' our day.

That is why travelling in a westward direction is more body-clock friendly than flying east. NASA studies of long haul pilots showed that westward travel was associated with significantly better sleep quantity and quality than eastward flights.

When flying west, you are 'extending' your day, thus travelling in the natural direction of your internal clock. Flying eastward will involve 'shrinking' or reducing your day and is in direct opposition to your internal clock's natural tendency.

One of the more common complaints of travellers is that their sleep becomes disrupted. There are many reasons for this: changing time zones and schedules, changing light and activity levels, trying to sleep when your body clock is programmed to be awake, disruption of the internal circadian clock and working longer hours.

Sleep loss, jet lag and fatigue can seriously affect our ability to function well. Judgement and decision-making can be reduced by 50%, attention by 75%, memory by 20% and communication by 30%.

It is often suggested that you adjust your watch as soon as you board a plane, supposedly to try to help you adjust to your destination's schedule as soon as you arrive. But it can take the body clock several days to several weeks to fully adjust to a new time zone.

So, our body clock truly can 'govern' us.

**2** **exam task** For questions 1–6, choose the answer (**A, B, C** or **D**) which you think fits best according to the text.

1 The main function of the body clock is to
   - **A** help us sleep.
   - **B** help us adapt to a 24-hour cycle.
   - **C** regulate the body's functions.
   - **D** govern all the body's responses.

2 Jet lag
   - **A** causes our body clock to change.
   - **B** makes our body clock operate badly.
   - **C** extends the hours of our body clock.
   - **D** upsets our body's rhythms.

**3** The direction you fly in

   A  helps you sleep better.

   B  affects the degree of jet lag.

   C  extends or shrinks your body clock.

   D  alters your body's natural rhythms.

**4** According to the article

   A  flying seriously affects our judgement and decision-making.

   B  various factors stop us sleeping when we fly.

   C  jet lag can affect different abilities differently.

   D  travellers complain about the negative effects of flying.

**5** On the subject of avoiding jet lag the article

   A  makes no suggestions.

   B  suggests changing the time on your watch.

   C  proposes gradually adjusting your body clock.

   D  says there is nothing you can do.

**6** The tone of this article is

   A  rather dramatic.

   B  quite serious.

   C  very scientific.

   D  persuasive.

**3** Collocations

Complete these collocations as used in the article.

1 body ...................................

2 afternoon ...................................

3 biological ...................................

4 jet ...................................

5 24 ...................................

6 time ...................................

## Writing

**1** Here is a letter written by a girl on behalf of her family. (NB The letter contains some language mistakes.) Read the letter and then answer these questions:

1 Why did she write the letter?

2 Who is the letter written to?

3 Is the letter written in formal or informal language?
Note down at least three examples to support your answer.

---

Dear ........................,

I am writing on behalf of my parents, my sister and myself to do a serious complaint about the holiday we recently went on that was organise by your firm.

   Since we (my parents, my sister and myself) returned from holiday we were seriously ill by food poisoning. We began feeling ill as soon as we returned home and my parents couldn't return to work on the following Monday. Later that week as we were all feeling very sick, we went to the doctor, which confirmed that we had food poisoning. We have been ill since a fortnight, and I am the only one who is now beginning to feel a little better and strong enough to do things like as write this letter.

   We are sure that we got the food poisoning while stay at the 'Happy Hotel' that your firm booked for us. We didn't eat anywhere except at the hotel while we were on holiday because we had full board at the hotel, as you can check. Also, while we were staying at the hotel, we became concerned about the hygiene there. My sister noticed lots of cockroaches in and near the kitchen. I once found an insect in my supper and nothing smelt or looked like very clean. Also, there was no water during two days.

   We wish to claim compensation from your firm for all the illness and inconvenience that we have suffered. We feel that as we are sick for over a fortnight but were only on holiday for a week, your firm must to reimburse us for the cost of the whole holiday.

   We look forward to hearing from you, and to receiving compensation.

   Yours sincerely,

---

**2** There are five paragraphs in this letter. Why? What is the function of each paragraph and how is the letter organised?

**3** Note down the expressions used in the letter that are typical of a transactional letter of complaint.

**4** This letter is only a first draft. It contains 12 language mistakes which need to be corrected before the letter can be sent. Find them and correct them.

# Grammar

**1** Do you use a mobile phone? Do you think they are safe for your health?
What does this doctor think?

Mobile phones (0) ..C. microwave radio emissions. Researchers are questioning whether exposure to these radiowaves might (1) ..... to brain cancer.

So far, the data are not conclusive. The scientific evidence does not (2) ..... us to say with certainty that mobile phones are categorically (3) ..... .
On the other hand, current research has not yet (4) ..... clear adverse effects associated with the prolonged use of mobile phones.

Numerous studies are now going (5) ..... in various countries. Some of the results are contradictory but others have shown an association between mobile phone use and cancer. (6) ..... , these studies are preliminary and the issue needs further, long-term investigation.

(7) ..... the scientific data are more definite, it is prudent for people to try not to use mobile phones for long (8) ..... of time. Don't think that hands-free phones are any safer either. At the moment, research is in fact showing the (9) ..... and they may be just as dangerous.

It is also thought that young people (10) ..... bodies are still growing may be at particular risk.

**2** **exam task** Read the article again and decide which answer **A, B, C** or **D** best fits each space. There is an example at the beginning (0).

| | | | | |
|---|---|---|---|---|
| 0 | **A** send | **B** give | **C** emit | **D** charge |
| 1 | **A** cause | **B** lead | **C** produce | **D** bring |
| 2 | **A** enable | **B** make | **C** able | **D** let |
| 3 | **A** risky | **B** secure | **C** unhealthy | **D** safe |
| 4 | **A** proved | **B** demonstrated | **C** caused | **D** produced |
| 5 | **A** by | **B** on | **C** through | **D** about |
| 6 | **A** Though | **B** Additionally | **C** However | **D** While |
| 7 | **A** Provide | **B** As | **C** When | **D** Until |
| 8 | **A** amounts | **B** periods | **C** quantities | **D** intervals |
| 9 | **A** fact | **B** opposite | **C** way | **D** truth |
| 10 | **A** as | **B** that | **C** with | **D** whose |

**3** What makes you stressed? How do you try to overcome stress?
Think about your answers to these questions, then read the text below
and decide which word: *very, too, so* or *such* to put in each space.

### SOME GOLDEN TIPS FOR MANAGING STRESS

- Notice what makes you feel (1) .............................. anxious. Face your anxieties.

- See what you can change in those areas where you are doing (2) ............................ much.

- Are you overreacting to things? Is it necessary to get (3) .............................
upset/anxious/angry?

- Are you breathing (4) .............................. fast? Slow, deep breathing helps you relax.

- Try using some relaxation techniques such as yoga or biofeedback. They can be
(5) .............................. useful in helping you relax.

- Get strong! Make sure you're not (6) ............................. fat. Don't drink (7) ........................... much
coffee or alcohol.  Do you need to smoke (8) ............................. much or even at all? Exercise
three or four times a week, but don't exercise (9) ........................... much.
It can be bad for you.

- Don't forget your friends. They can give you (10) ............................ valuable support
and help, as you can to them.

## Vocabulary

**1** exam task For questions **1–10**, read the text below. Use the word given in
capitals at the end of each line to form a word that fits in the
space in the same line. There is an example at the beginning (0).

| | |
|---|---|
| **MOBILE PHONES MAKE (0)** ..*owners*.. **FAT** | **OWN** |
| It may be a status symbol, but carrying a mobile phone makes you fat and is helping to fuel an **(1)** ..... in obesity, Dr Andrew Prentice, a nutritional expert has warned. | **EXPLODE** |
| A mobile phone robs a person of 16 kilometres a year of **(2)** ..... , Dr Prentice told the British **(3)** ..... of Science, at Leeds University, England. | **WALK** <br> **ASSOCIATE** |
| He added that, in **(4)** ..... with all the other aspects of a lazy modern **(5)** ..... such as TV 'zappers', powersteering, escalators and lifts, the mobile phone was at least **(6)** ..... to blame for the 'startling' increase in the number of people who have become grossly **(7)** ...... . | **COMBINE** <br> **STYLE** <br> **PART** <br> **WEIGH** |
| During this century the average **(8)** ..... of adults in Britain has increased by almost 10 kilograms, and the number of **(9)** ..... obese people has more than doubled since 1980, Dr Prentice said. | **WEIGH** <br> **OFFICIAL** |
| Yet another warning that these wonderful devices also have their **(10)** ...... . | **ADVANTAGE** |

**2** Complete this table by filling in the corresponding noun for each of the verbs, as in the example.

| Verb | Noun |
|------|------|
| to invent | *invention* |
| to diagnose | |
| to inject | |
| to operate | |
| to treat | |
| to cure | |
| to injure | |
| to infect | |
| to sweat | |

**3** Label the parts of the body on the photograph. Which parts of the body do these adjectives often collocate with?

bony   long   shiny   bright   firm
rough   smooth   flat   muscly

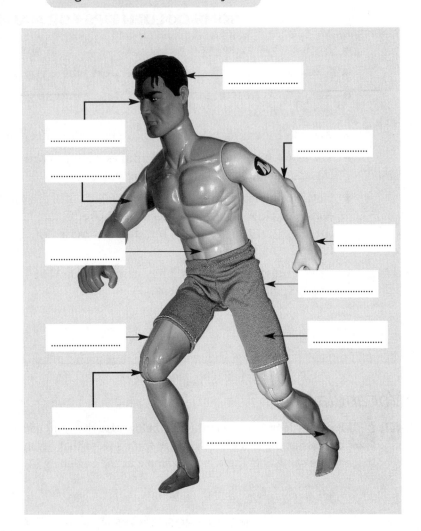

# Preparation for speaking

**1** In class your teacher will ask you to talk about one of these topics:

- Describe an illness you once had (your symptoms, the treatment, etc.)
- Are modern lifestyles bad for our health?

Choose one of the topics, and get ready to talk for about two minutes about it, by noting down your opinions, and thinking about what language you will want to use. Your teacher may ask you to speak about the topic as part of a mini-presentation or in a discussion.

**2** Can you distinguish between these two sounds: /i/ (as in 'hit') and /iː/ (as in 'heat')? Look at this set of words in which the two sounds are contrasted and practise saying them out loud.

hit / heat    it / eat    bit / beat    lip / leap
fit / feet    knit / neat    sit / seat    lid / lead

Can you think of any other words in English that are just distinguished by these two sounds? Note down at least three pairs and bring them to class.

# Exam focus  Paper 1 Writing

## Parts 1 and 2 Letters

**1** **Part 1 Letter**

**exam task** You have seen this information about an adventure course in Scotland. It interests you as it could be good for your physical fitness, your self-esteem, your independence and your interpersonal skills, as well as being fun. But you need lots more information before making up your mind.

Read the information and the notes you have made, then write a letter of enquiry covering all the points in your notes and any other relevant information. Your letter should be between **120–180** words and written in an appropriate style.

**2** **Part 2 Letter**

**exam task** You have had a miserable holiday. You broke your leg on the first day and have had to spend your time in bed or resting. Write a letter to a friend explaining how you broke your leg, how you feel and what you have been doing to pass the time. Add any other relevant information too. Your letter should be **120–180** words and written in an appropriate style.

## EXPLORE

Age: 11--17 (sea) / 7-13 (land)   Length: 6 days

**Your chance to:**
- Enjoy a fun and exciting trip
- Feel good about who you are and what you do
- Live and work with others as a team
- Build up your physical fitness and endurance

If you're away from home for the first time, you may feel a little strange. Like many other participants on this course, you will findthis feeling soon gives way to excitement as you get actively involved in the many activities available.

*Where do we sleep?/ Accommodation?*

Throughout the course, a well-trained and friendly instructor will guide your work in small groups of five or six. Once you've completed the initial activities which involve team- and trust-building exercises, safety instructions, a life-jacket drill, and a water-confidence assessment, you will move on to a series of action-based training sessions.

*What if activities too difficult?*

Before heading back home, you will feel so proud that you have learned how to take care of yourself on a daily basis and how to cooperate with others.

*How long each day? Free time?*

### EXPLORE BY SEA COURSE

Participants will sail on 'The Odyssey' to some incredibly beautiful protected waters where they will take part in kayaking, hiking and camping.

*Price? What included? Same for sea and land courses?*

### EXPLORE BY LAND COURSE

This course is run at the Loch Headquarters. Participants will take part in rock climbing, kayaking, orienteering, hill walking and camping.

*Application form?*

# Entertainment

## Reading

**1** This text is about the New York club scene. Think about nightclubs and what you usually find in them. Before you read, try to predict which word in the first list will be used with which word in the second list. Then, as you read the text, check to see if you were right.

> latest    techno    dance
> designer    sound    leather
> fashion-    trendy

> system    floor    beat
> conscious    outfits
> set    clothes    craze

**2** **exam task** Choose the most suitable heading from the list A–I for each part (1–7) of the article. There is one extra heading which you do not need to use. There is an example at the beginning (0).

**A** Evidence of change

**B** Losing yourself in foam

**C** You can still look great

**D** Foam makes its appearance

**E** Not just for teenagers

**F** A way round common problems

**G** Being cool in foam

**H** Appealing to the senses

**I** Figures in foam

## Bubbles hit the floor

*We've had disco, rave and lambada, but the latest club craze is the strangest. New York's glitterati are glistening in soap suds as they dance in 6ft of foam.*

| **0** | I |
|---|---|

A kid with a white Afro and a bubble beard vanishes in a sea of foam, accompanied by the latest techno beat. Meanwhile, other heads and bodies bob in and out of the soapy cloud, their hair unisexed by bubble styles. No, this is not an ad for instant cappuccino, but the latest craze to hit New York. Welcome to foam night at the Palladium, one of Manhattan's most popular clubs.

| **1** | |
|---|---|

What happens at a foam club is simply this: soapy bubbles – a secret mixture of baby shampoo, air and water – are blown onto the club's dance floor to create a slippery den where soapy young things can dance and splash around anonymously. The club's sound system, however, is protected from this chaos by being raised up on a platform.

| **2** | |
|---|---|

The craze for foam-filled nightclubs currently sweeping the city began as so many fads in the club world do, in Ibiza, Spain. From there it spread across Europe (in France, a foam night is known as a *soirée mousse*) and to New York, where foam clubs seem to be springing up on every corner. The actual idea for foam clubs, though, apparently has its origins in the 1992 Barcelona Olympics, where foam jets were used in the opening ceremony.

| **3** | |
|---|---|

For the equivalent of around just £12 Manhattan's Palladium, Tunnel and Limelight clubs all offer the chance to wriggle around in waist-high bubbles. Each of the clubs attracts a different clientele. At the Palladium, teenagers bounce around in shorts and vests. At the Limelight it ranges from kids who slip through the door to men in suits or even the occasional curious tourist. At the Tunnel, it's the seriously trendy set.

**4**

Actors, models and the hopelessly fashion-conscious no longer stand around but spend most of the night bopping around on one dance floor and then, when the heat is too much, they move down to the other in the foam. Juliette Lewis, Leonardo DiCaprio, Prince and Naomi Campbell are all known to hang out here.

**5**

And apparently you needn't worry about your designer clothes, either. Although it would be a good idea to leave any suede or leather outfits at home, anything else should be fine. The bubbles are dry to the touch, but leave a slimy trace that evaporates in seconds. The only risk is of smudging your mascara or losing the shine on your shoes.

**6**

When I went to the Palladium last week, the bubbles smelt strongly of washing-up liquid but the club's owner told me that he usually adds a little vanilla or rose essence. 'Cosmetics companies often call me up,' he said 'asking me to organise parties where the scent of their choice is put into the foam.'

**7**

As the Palladium released its tired patrons as dawn broke over New York last week, rather than the usual trail of empty bottles and cigarette packs, I saw instead the extraordinary sight of long streams of bubbles floating on the early morning air. Exhausted, but seemingly happy, the foam bathers were finally heading home.

**3** **exam task** Read the article again. For questions **1–4**, choose the answer (**A**, **B**, **C** or **D**) which you think fits best according to the text.

1 According to the text, foam would be good for promoting
  A instant cappuccino.
  B perfume.
  C vanilla.
  D unisex hairstyles.

2 According to the text, Ibiza
  A was an unusual place for foam nights to start.
  B stole the idea from France.
  C was second to Barcelona in introducing foam clubs.
  D is an important place in the 'club' world.

3 According to the writer, clubs with foam in New York
  A are relatively expensive.
  B appeal mainly to kids.
  C are opening everywhere.
  D will not become popular.

4 In the writer's view foam will encourage clubbers to
  A dance more.
  B go to regular clubs.
  C dress more casually.
  D drink and smoke more.

**4** Without looking back at the text, complete this table.

| Noun | Adjective | Verb | Noun |
|------|-----------|------|------|
| curiosity | curious | mix | |
| trend | | originate | |
| soap | | heat | |
| slip | | own | |
| | chaotic | choose | |

Now check your answers by finding the words in the text.

# Writing

**1** Look at this question and some extracts from students' letters that were written in response. Decide which students have responded appropriately.

> You are spending the summer at an English language school in Britain and would like to organise the showing of a series of films for your fellow students. You know that the school has strict rules about after school activities and that you need to write to the principal to ask permission. Using the notes you have made on the left and considering the information on the right, write a letter to the principal.
>
> - Four Friday evenings in July/Aug.
> - Caretaker available
> - Use activity room
> - English language films
> - Staff will open coffee shop
>
> **Student Activities:** Students wishing to hold activities at the school should write to request permission a week in advance. Requests will only be considered where the caretaker is available to open and close the school and where the activity is of cultural value to the students attending.

**a** Dear Principal,
I would like to show some films at the school.
I hope this is OK with you.

**b** The activity room with all that space is a good place.

**c** The staff at the coffee shop have agreed to open and run the shop on these evenings.

**d** *Fridays in August and July are good for us. What about you?*

**e** You tell me if the caretaker is available.

**f** I know that many students will enjoy these films and find them interesting.

**g** I know there are rules about student activities so don't worry because we will follow them.

**h** I hate those American action films with all that violence.

**i** *Dear Mrs Jones,
I am writing to ask your permission to show a number of English language films in the evenings after school.*

**j** If I can get the keys, I'll be able to open and close the building myself.

**2** Write out your own full version of the letter. You can include the best bits from the extracts. Bring your letter to class to discuss with other students.

# Grammar

**1** Complete the gap in each sentence using between one and three words with the correct present tense form of the verb in brackets.

1 I ........................... . Can we move to another seat? (not hear)

2 I ........................... here just until I find my own place. (stay)

3 It ........................... good. What are you cooking? (smell)

4 He ........................... a shower. Can I get him to call you back? (have)

5 They ........................... us much because it's such a long way to travel. (not visit)

6 It's very sad. I ........................... things were different but they're not. (wish)

7 The stadium ........................... up to 30,000 spectators. (hold)

8 He's usually very tired. He ........................... home until midnight sometimes. (not get)

9 I think things ........................... out of control. We'd better leave just to be safe. (get)

10 What ........................... you? You don't seem interested in the film. (bother)

11 It ........................... at least £15 million to make a Hollywood film these days. (cost)

12 They ........................... far too many violent films on TV nowadays. (show)

Now match one of the grammar explanations from the list to each sentence to show why you used the particular form of a verb.

a temporary situation
b verb of perception
c action 'around' time of speaking
d general truth
e permanent situation
f habitual action
g verb of emotional state
h developing situation

**2** In this text about windsurfing there are 12 highlighted words connected with the theme of leisure. The wrong form of the word has been used in each case. Write down the correct form of each word.

Now an Olympic sport, windsurfing is a naturally **(1)** compete sport and there are all sorts of **(2)** competes for the ambitious. Once the **(3)** basic have been mastered, most boardsailors aim for faster speeds. It's not until you've sailed at 'planing' speed (skimming the water's surface in a high wind) that you fully appreciate the **(4)** thriller potential of windsurfing. If you're **(5)** in competing, most clubs run informal racing events, a good place to start.

Windsurfing is not **(6)** expense, and even when you've learnt to sail there's no need to rush out and buy a board. Most **(7)** equipping can be hired; at some hotels and resorts it is supplied at no extra **(8)** costing to their guests as part of the holiday.

This is a **(9)** funny sport for everyone to **(10)** enjoyable, regardless of age or sex, whether it's a family **(11)** fool around on a sunny beach in Spain, an **(12)** enthusiastic racing at the local club, or an advanced high speed aerial merchant challenging the strong winds in Hawaii.

**3**  **exam task** Read the text below and look carefully at each line. Some of the lines are correct and some have a word which should not be there. If a line is correct, put a tick (✓) by it. If a line has a word which should not be there, write the word at the end of the line. There are two examples at the beginning (0 and 00).

| | | |
|---|---|---|
| **0** | TV has changed so a lot lately. There are hundreds of soap operas and series | so |
| **00** | on all the time. TV programmers obviously believe the way to get you to watch | ✓ |
| **1** | more is being to put on a series. They are probably right. I know from my family | |
| **2** | that the most evenings someone will say that they can't go out or do something | |
| **3** | because their 'soap' is on. People make appointments with the TV and usually | |
| **4** | end up watching programmes that are shown before and after their particular | |
| **5** | favourite. My brother is the worst because he doesn't care what he watches at. | |
| **6** | He has his favourite programmes but he often sits for hours just changing | |
| **7** | channels with the remote control before they do come on. Even the adverts are | |
| **8** | something which he enjoys himself. He sometimes calls me into the room to | |
| **9** | see an advert which he finds it amusing. I suppose you could say that he is | |
| **10** | addicted to TV but it is different from other addictions. For example, when we | |
| **11** | currently go on holiday he is very happy to do other things. He doesn't think | |
| **12** | for a minute about the episodes he might be missing. There must be something | |
| **13** | very relaxing about watching TV which makes him to sit for so long at home | |
| **14** | and flick from one channel to another. The worrying thing is that it is not just | |
| **15** | young people who waste of their days in this way. It can in fact be people | |
| | of almost any age. | |

# Vocabulary

**1** When making vocabulary notes on verbs, it is a good idea to note down the different patterns that can follow the verb and to write down some examples.

EXAMPLE: *can't stand (object)*
*(verb + -ing)*
*I can't stand horror films.*
*He can't stand people talking about him.*
*I can't stand having to rush.*

Here are some more verbs that you have seen in the language sections in the Student's Book in this unit. Make similar notes for these verbs, including a note on particular uses with prepositions where necessary.

> keep    spend (time)
> spend (money)    waste (time)
> appeal    enjoy

**2** **exam task** For questions 1–12, read the text below. Use the word given in capitals at the end of each line to form a word that fits in the space in the same line. There is an example at the beginning (0).

## SPORT IN ITALY

Football is by far the most important sport in Italy, (0) *uniting*    UNITE
the country when the (1) ..... team (Azzurri) play. The football    NATION
season, (2) ..... from September through to June, culminates    RUN
with the final of the *Coppa Italia* (3) ..... , the equivalent    COMPETE
of the English FA Cup. Italy's football (4) ..... ,  however,    OBSESS
reaches a climax (5) ..... every four years when the World Cup    ONE
is (6) ..... .  Other sports throughout the year also attract    HOLD
a large (7) ..... , so fans are never at a loss for varied    FOLLOW
(8) ...... .  For most big sporting events, tickets can be obtained    ACTIVE
for cash at club outlets such as the venue itself. (9) .....  provide    AGENT
hard-to-get tickets but often at (10) ..... prices. Beware of buying    INFLATE
(11) ..... tickets from touts at popular events as their expensive    ENTER
tickets may be (12) ..... .    VALID

---

# Preparation for speaking

**1** Look at the short responses in the list below. Which ones could be possible responses to the statements made by Speaker A? In some cases more than one response is possible.

> **a** Whereabouts?    **b** Like what?    **c** So what?    **d** How come?
> **e** Why else?    **f** Never mind.    **g** Why not?    **h** Please do.

**Speaker A**                                                    **Speaker B (response)**

1  Is it all right if I bring a friend?                          ...............

2  I won't be able to make it now.                               ...............

3  There are loads of things to do there.                       ...............

4  You're not going just to see him.                            ...............

5  Let's meet in town later.                                     ...............

6  We're not allowed to play music so late.                     ...............

7  I know a great club we could go to.                          ...............

8  There were several problems while making the film.           ...............

**2** Imagine that you have the equivalent of £10 to spend. Find an advertisement in English (from a magazine, the Internet, etc.) for an entertainment event or product that you think is good value. Make notes on what you find under the following headings:

*Event or product*
*Particular features*
*Appeal (who to?)*
*Value for money?*

Bring your notes and the advertisement (if possible) to class and try to convince another student that what you have found represents good value for money.

# *Exam focus* **Paper 3 Use of English**

## Part 1 Multiple-choice cloze

Looking back at the vocabulary work you have done in the Student's Book will help you to complete this exam task successfully.

In doing this task, follow these steps:

1 Read the text through first to get a good idea of what it is about.

2 Read each sentence where there is a space carefully two or three times.

3 Think about what kind of word you are looking for, e.g. adjective or adverb, countable or uncountable noun.

4 Find reasons to eliminate the three wrong answers before selecting the one you think is right.

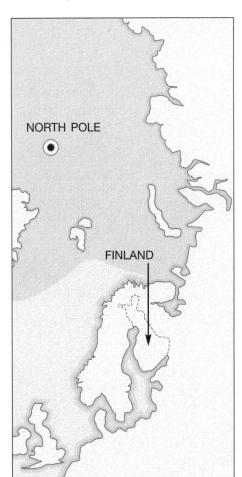

NORTH POLE

FINLAND

 For questions **1–15**, read the text below and decide which answer **A, B, C** or **D** best fits each space. There is an example at the beginning **(0)**.

### LONG SUMMER NIGHTS

I was in Vaasa for a midsummer music **(0)** .C., Ranta Rock. It was just one of dozens of festivals taking **(1)** ..... around the country on the longest day of the year. Finns **(2)** ..... their summer pleasure seriously. So would you if it only **(3)** ..... three months, and the rest of the year was **(4)** ..... freezing in near-constant darkness. Given its high latitude, Finland **(5)** ..... long, severe winters and short, cool summers. It does, **(6)** ....., get a lot of summer daylight and everyone **(7)** ..... their best to squeeze as much action into those **(8)** ..... hours as they can.

On any summer weekend in Finland there are usually 10 to 15 music festivals. But on this **(9)** ..... weekend, there are as many as 50. All around the country, to **(10)** ..... the longest days, adults retire to their summer cottages, while the nation's **(11)** ..... go to music festivals. Finland has been **(12)** ..... as mainland Scandinavia's most **(13)** ..... isolated and least understood country and to begin to understand it you have to **(14)** ..... these special summer nights. At midnight, the sky **(15)** ..... red, pink and orange with the most glorious sunset.

| 0 | A feast | B rock | C festival | D reunion |
|---|---------|--------|------------|-----------|
| 1 | A part | B up | C place | D forward |
| 2 | A hold | B take | C think | D amuse |
| 3 | A lasted | B happened | C took | D came |
| 4 | A used | B spent | C made | D held |
| 5 | A suffers | B belongs | C passes | D spends |
| 6 | A whereas | B on the contrary | C however | D on the other hand |
| 7 | A makes | B amuses | C enjoys | D does |
| 8 | A plenty | B more | C further | D extra |
| 9 | A particular | B single | C occasional | D contemporary |
| 10 | A celebrate | B amuse | C congratulate | D entertain |
| 11 | A infants | B youth | C childhood | D youngster |
| 12 | A said | B called | C described | D compared |
| 13 | A far | B culturally | C long | D enjoyably |
| 14 | A experience | B appeal | C pass | D attend |
| 15 | A lit | B shone | C turned | D came |

# Science and technology

## Reading

**1** Many people say that time spent playing computer and video games is wasted time. What do you think? Read through the article below. What does it say about this?

### COMPUTER FUN 'GOOD FOR YOUNG BRAINS'

It looks as though many young people may have some good news coming their way. **0** **G** Scientists say the games, far from being bad for adolescents, actually help them develop their skills of concentration, 'visualisation' and problem-solving.

**1** [ ] The results of a study of about 200 students in America and Italy were recently published in the *Journal of Applied Developmental Psychology.* **2** [ ]

There is further evidence too. **3** [ ] Scholar J.C. Herz, of Harvard University, said: 'Video games are perfect training for life in transitional America where daily existence demands the ability to arrange 16 kinds of information being fired at you simultaneously from telephones, televisions, fax machines, pagers, personal digital assistants, voice messaging systems, postal delivery, e-mail and the Internet. **4** [ ]. Those to the joystick born have a built-in advantage.'

Such statements would have been treated as heresy only five years ago by parents and teachers. **5** [ ]

**2** exam task Read the article again. Six sentences have been removed from it. Choose from the sentences A–G the one which fits each gap (1–5). There is one extra sentence which you do not need to use. There is an example at the beginning (0).

A There had been fears children would form a 'mindless addiction'.

B 'You have to recognise patterns in this whirl of data and you have to do it fast.'

C This goes against previously held beliefs.

D According to a report in the *New York Times*, some experts believe computer games are a contributing factor in the steady rise in IQ scores in the industrialised world.

E It seems that a youth 'misspent' in the company of computer games serves as useful grooming for a role in a high-technology economy.

F The researchers concluded that computer games should be seen as a form of intellectual exercise.

G A growing body of research in America suggests computer and video games may benefit young minds.

**3** Match the words on the left to their meanings on the right. It will help you if you first find the word in the article and try to work out its meaning.

| Words from the article | | Meanings as used in the article |
| --- | --- | --- |
| 1 | research | **a** belief which goes against accepted ones |
| 2 | benefit | **b** learning or practising skills |
| 3 | steady | **c** gradual |
| 4 | evidence | **d** a computer control sometimes shaped like a lever |
| 5 | training | **e** to communicate very rapidly and repeatedly |
| 6 | to fire | **f** very strong and constant need or desire for something |
| 7 | patterns | **g** be good for, help |
| 8 | joystick | **h** detailed study |
| 9 | heresy | **i** clues based on experience or information |
| 10 | addiction | **j** regularities, consistencies |

Now read the article again and think about the meaning of these words as you read it.

**4** Here is a list of points that summarise the article. Complete the gaps in the sentences. Try to do it without looking back at the article first. Then tick the statements that you agree with, and think of arguments to back up or prove your opinions. Be prepared to discuss these in class.

## Computer and video games

- Help children develop their (1) .......................... of concentration, visualisation and problem-solving.

- Have contributed to the steady (2) .......................... in IQ scores.

- (3) .......................... a kind of intellectual exercise.

- Train (4) .......................... to take up roles in high-technology societies.

- (5) .......................... young people to be able to handle information coming fast and from all directions.

- Give people practice in recognising (6) .......................... in rapidly delivered information.

**5** The third paragraph of the article mentions nine kinds of communication devices. List them, then check their meaning in a dictionary. Tick the ones you have and underline the ones you would like to have. Be prepared to discuss your answers in class.

**6** Try to play three different computer games before your next English class. As you do so, make a note of the kinds of skills they require you to use and the types of information they require you to handle.

**7** Five groups of words in the article and the sentences below it are highlighted. They all have something grammatical in common. What is it? Why is this form used in each of these cases?

# Writing

**1** Here is a letter of complaint. Read it to see what the complaint is about.

> Dear Sir or Madam,
>
> Last week I bought a computer by mail order from your company. I'd saved up for it for (1) ages and was (2) really pleased when it arrived. I (3) got everything going and everything worked (4) fine for about two hours, then suddenly it (5) just went dead on me and hasn't worked since.
>
> (6) I'm really fed up about this. Your company has (7) messed me around, and wasted my time and money. (8) I want a replacement computer or my money back (9) right away. Otherwise I'll have to (10) get in touch with the newspapers to complain.
>
> (11) Reply immediately please, or else.
>
> Yours faithfully,

**2** The style of this letter is both informal and rude. Because of this it probably wouldn't get a good reception from the computer company. The highlighted words and phrases are the ones that make the style 'inappropriate'. Below are some more neutral and appropriate ways of saying the same things. They are in jumbled order. Decide which one should replace each of the highlighted parts in the letter.

**a** I would like
**b** well
**c** a long time
**d** I would be grateful for your prompt attention to this matter, and look forward to hearing from you shortly.
**e** very
**f** stopped working
**g** caused me considerable inconvenience
**h** This is most disappointing
**i** installed it
**j** contact
**k** immediately

**3** **exam task** You have received through the post a hi-tech tent that you ordered. However, part of it is damaged and the assembly instructions are very complicated. As a result, you can't use it for your holiday and may have to make other holiday plans.

Write a letter of complaint to the mail order company in which you explain the problem and the inconvenience you have been caused, and ask for some form of compensation. Your letter should be **120–180** words long and written in an appropriate style.

Use the language in **1** and **2** to help you with the letter.

# Grammar

**1** Read the text below. It is about how medical science helped some babies born with severe medical problems.

**2** [exam task] Read the text again and look carefully at each line. Some of the lines are correct, and some have a word which should not be there. If a line is correct, put a tick (✓) at the end of the line. If a line has a word that should **not** be there, write the word at the end of the line. There are two examples at the beginning (**0** and **00**).

| | | |
|---|---|---|
| **0** | Parents often worry that there will be 'something wrong' with their new babies. | ✓ |
| **00** | Here are two examples of things that they did go wrong, both, fortunately with | they |
| **1** | happy endings. In 1977 a four-legged boy was born at a hospital in England. | |
| **2** | He was then moved him to another hospital. After six weeks, doctors carried out the | |
| **3** | rare and delicate operation of removing his handicap. According to newspaper | |
| **4** | reports of 22 March of that year the operation was a success well and the | |
| **5** | child he was doing well. | |
| **6** | Here's the second example. In 1982, a child was born in the United States with a | |
| **7** | bullet in his brain. His 17-year-old mother had gave birth to the boy more than | |
| **8** | two months prematurely after she was being shot in a love-triangle quarrel. The | |
| **9** | bullet passed through her lower back and through her kidney before it lodging in the | |
| **10** | brain of the unborn child. The boy, Daniel, was delivered by Caesarean section several | |
| **11** | of hours later. He was put on a life support system and it was two months | |
| **12** | before the operating team at Broward General Hospital in Florida felt be able to | |
| **13** | remove the bullet. The doctor, who was supervised the operation, said the baby | |
| **14** | was born in a bad condition and he felt pretty certain he would die. His recovery and | |
| **15** | survival instinct had been very quite remarkable. Later reports stated that | |
| **16** | Daniel was now being a perfectly normal toddler. | |

There are four examples of the passive form in the text.
Find them and underline them.  Why are they used?

**3** [exam task] Complete the second sentence so that it has a similar meaning to the first sentence, using the word given. **Do not change the word given.** You must use between two and five words, including the word given. Here is an example.

EXAMPLE:
The article gives two examples of stories with happy endings.
**are**

Two stories with happy endings **are given in** the article.

1 Someone shot Daniel's mother while she was pregnant.
**was**
Daniel's mother ............................ pregnant.

2 The papers reported that a four-legged boy was born.
**reported**
It ............................ four-legged boy had been born.

3 They removed a bullet from the baby's brain.
**had**
The baby ............................ his brain.

4 The doctors gave the mother a Caesarean section.
**was**
The mother ............................ section.

5 After he was born they moved the baby to another hospital.
**was**
After he was born ............................ another hospital.

6 They say the baby was born with four legs.
**said**
The baby ............................ born with four legs.

## Vocabulary

**1** **exam task** Read the text below. Use the word given in capitals at the end of the lines to form a word that fits in the space in the same line. There is an example at the beginning (0).

### A SURPRISING WAY OF CHANGING YOUR ACCENT

A woman who went to bed with a
(0) .Scottish. accent but woke up sounding        **SCOTLAND**
South African is casting new light on a rare
condition. Foreign accent syndrome has been
(1) ..... no more than a dozen times this          **REPORT**
century, and follows (2) ..... to the brain caused **INJURE**
by stroke or accident. It is a highly (3) .....     **USUAL**
condition. The voice changes in intonation and
(4) ..... , creating a different accent. An         **EMPHASISE**
American man (5) ..... in a car crash in 1994       **INVOLVE**
walked away with a French accent, but had
never (6) ..... to France. The woman who            **BE**
developed a South African accent woke up one
morning feeling dizzy and a stroke was (7) ..... .  **DIAGNOSIS**
She had lost her Scottish accent (8) ..... .        **NIGHT**

A scan showed the left side of her brain had
undergone damage. It is this area which
controls the mechanisms of (9) ..... , said Dr      **SPEAK**
Sophie Scott, of the Applied Psychology Unit
in Cambridge, who is a principal (10) ..... on      **RESEARCH**
the case.

**2** Label all the parts in this picture.
Use a dictionary to help you if you need to.

## Preparation for speaking

**1** In class your teacher will ask you to talk on these topics:

**a** Compare and contrast these two different CD players. Which one would you prefer to own and why?

**b** What are the advantages and disadvantages of sound systems and portable CD players?

Get ready to talk for about two minutes on each topic, by noting down your opinions, and thinking about what language you will want to use. Your teacher may ask you to speak about the topic as part of a mini-presentation or in a discussion.

**2** Can you distinguish between these two sounds: /æ/ (as in 'hat') and /ʌ/ (as in 'hut')? Look at this set of words in which the two sounds are contrasted and practise saying them out loud.

| | | |
|---|---|---|
| hat / hut | bat / but | lack / luck |
| sack / suck | mad / mud | |
| bag / bug | cap / cup | crash / crush |

Can you think of any other words in English that are just distinguished by these two sounds? Note down at least three pairs and bring them to class.

# Exam focus  Paper 4 Listening

In the FCE exam, Paper 4 is the Listening paper. It is quite easy to prepare for the other exam papers and the skills they require at home. But how can you improve your listening skills outside class? Here are some suggestions. Which ones could work for you? Be ready to discuss your answers in class.

Look at page 55 in the Student's Book. Which of the suggestions below could help you with which part of the Listening paper?

## IMPROVING MY LISTENING SKILLS OUTSIDE CLASS

| | SUGGESTIONS | WHAT ABOUT YOU? |
|---|---|---|
| 1 | Watch films/videos in English | Can you do this?<br>How?<br>Where?<br>Names of favourite films?<br>Problems? |
| 2 | Listen to tourists or friends speaking English/speak with them | Can you do this?<br>How?<br>Where?<br>Problems? |
| 3 | Speak to friends from your country in English | Can you do this?<br>How?<br>Where?<br>Talk about what?<br>Problems? |
| 4 | Tune in to programmes in English | Can you do this?<br>How?<br>What channels?<br>Favourite programmes?<br>Problems? |
| 5 | Download radio programmes on your computer in English | Can you do this?<br>What web addresses?<br>Favourite programmes?<br>Problems? |
| 6 | Watch TV programmes in English | Can you do this?<br>What channels?<br>Favourite programmes?<br>Problems? |
| 7 | Listen to recordings of stories, plays, etc. in English. | Can you do this?<br>How?<br>Favourites?<br>Problems? |
| 8 | Listen to songs in English | Can you do this?<br>Favourites?<br>Problems? |
| 9 | What else? | Make some suggestions |

# 5 Travel and tourism

## Reading

**1** Writers do not always express their attitudes or opinions directly in texts. Sometimes you will have to work out what a writer's feelings or views are from what he or she says indirectly.

Look at the first two paragraphs in the text and the dictionary definitions below. Underline the phrase or line which tells you:

a The writer is not looking forward to the journey.

b The writer is not feeling well.

c Almost everyone owns a car in the United States.

---

**hung-o•ver** /ɛˌhʌŋˈəʊ·vəʳ, $-ˈoʊ·və/ adj [after v] feeling ill with a bad pain in the head and often wanting to vomit after having drunk too much alcohol • *That was a great party last night, but I'm (feeling) really hung-over this morning* • See also HANGOVER ILLNESS .

---

**schiz•oid** /ˈskɪt·sɔɪd/ n, adj medical (a person who is) suffering from or behaving as if suffering from SCHIZOPHRENIA • *schizoid behaviour* • *a schizoid personality* • *The stress of fighting in the war turned him into a schizoid.* [C]

---

**short•com•ing** /ɛˈʃɔːtˌkʌm·ɪŋ, $ ˈʃɔːrt-, ˌ-ˈ--/ n [C usually pl] a failure to reach a particular standard • *Whatever his shortcomings as a husband, I think he was a good father to his children.* • *Like any political system, it has its shortcomings.*

---

**mis•giv•ing** /mɪsˈgɪv·ɪŋ-/ n a feeling of doubt, uncertainty or worry about a future event • *Many teachers have expressed serious misgivings about the new exams.* [C] • *My only misgiving is that we might not have enough time to do the job properly.* [C] • *The plan seemed to be utterly impractical and I was filled with misgiving about it.* [U]

---

**drool** /druːl/ v [I] to produce too much liquid in the mouth so that it flows out, or *(fig.)* to show extreme and sometimes foolish pleasure • *She brought with her an enormous dog that lay drooling on the mat.* • *(fig.) Roz and I sat by the swimming pool, drooling over all the gorgeous young men.* • *(fig.) I left Sara in the shop drooling over a green silk dress.* • *(fig.) I can sit for hours, drooling over recipes for rich chocolate cakes and desserts.*

---

## FIVE HOURS TO NEW YORK

It was ten minutes to seven in the morning and it was cold. Standing outside the Bloomsburg bus station, I could see my breath. I was hung-over and in a few minutes I was going to climb onto a bus for a five-hour ride to New York. I would sooner have eaten cat food. You only go on a long-distance bus in the United States because either you can't afford to fly or – and this is really licking the bottom of the barrel in America – you cannot afford a car. Being unable to afford a car in America is the last step before living out of a plastic sack. As a result, most of the people on long-distance buses are one of the following: actively schizoid, armed and dangerous, in a drugged stupor, just released from prison, or nuns. Occasionally you will also see a pair of Norwegian students. You can tell they are Norwegian students because they are so pink-faced and healthy-looking and they wear little blue ankle socks with their sandals. But by and large a ride on a long-distance bus in America combines most of the shortcomings of prison life with those of an ocean crossing on a troop-ship.

So when the bus pulled up before me, heaving a pneumatic sigh, and its doors flapped open, I boarded with some misgivings. The driver himself didn't appear any too stable. He had the sort of hair that made him appear as if he'd been playing with live wires. There were about half a dozen other passengers, though only two of them looked seriously insane and just one was talking to himself. I took a seat near the back and settled down to get some sleep.

When I awoke there was drool on my shoulder and a new passenger next to me, a haggard woman with lank grey hair who was chain-smoking and burping. They were the sort of burps children make to amuse themselves – rich, resonant burps. The woman was completely unself-conscious about it. She would look at me, open her mouth and out would roll a burp. It was amazing. Then she would take a drag on her cigarette and burp a large puff of smoke. That was amazing too. I stared out of the window, feeling ill, and tried to imagine circumstances less unpleasant than this. But apart from being dead or at a Bee Gees concert I couldn't think of a single thing.

39

**2** **exam task** Read the text. For questions 1–6, choose the answer (A, B, C or D) which you think fits best according to the text.

1  People generally travel on long-distance buses in America because

   A  it is often the only form of public transport.
   B  they are poor.
   C  they want to avoid driving.
   D  there are reduced fares for certain kinds of people.

2  In the writer's view a bus trip in America is similar to life in prison and on a troop-ship because of

   A  the time it takes.
   B  the level of comfort.
   C  the other passengers.
   D  the fact that everyone looks fit.

3  While outside the bus station, the writer was

   A  queuing by the bus doors.
   B  looking at his bus.
   C  waiting for his bus to come.
   D  looking for his departure point.

4  The writer's first impression of the driver was that he could be

   A  unsuitable for the job.
   B  a mechanic as well.
   C  feeling ill.
   D  the only stable person on the bus.

5  In the writer's opinion the woman passenger next to him

   A  was embarrassed about burping.
   B  tried to control herself by smoking.
   C  was behaving like a child.
   D  didn't care about other people's feelings.

6  'this' in line 39 refers to

   A  the view from the window.
   B  being dead or at a Bee Gees concert.
   C  feeling ill.
   D  the situation on the bus.

**3** In the text there are a number of personal nouns – nouns which describe types of people, e.g. *passenger*, *driver*. Common endings for these types of noun are *-er*, *-or* and *-ist*. Look at this list of words connected with travel and write the personal noun for each one under these headings.

| -er | -or | -ist |
| --- | --- | --- |

travel  operate  visit  motor  survive  cycle  tour
compete  hitch-hike  reception  instruct  camp

## Writing

**1** Here are parts of two letters written between friends. Jean's letter was written and sent first and Carol's (on page 34) is a reply. The highlighted parts of Jean's letter indicate what she would like to know from Carol. The highlighted parts of Carol's letter indicate where she is responding to a particular piece of news from Jean.

You should be able to fill in the missing parts of each letter by looking at what was written in the other one. Complete each letter and try to maintain the friendly and informal tone.

Dear Carol,

I know it's been ages since I last wrote but I've been very busy with school.

Let me know your plans and whether there's any chance we can meet up somewhere.

I'm seriously thinking about taking a year out before college and trying to see a bit of the world first. I've got no idea where I'd go, what I'd do or how I'd pay for it but that's what makes it such fun.

Anyway, don't leave it as long as I have and get back to me with possible dates for getting together and all your news.

Love,
Jean

Dear Jean,

It was great to hear from you. Busy or not you must find time to write. Friends like me live on news and gossip. Anyway, I was pleased to hear that your exams went smoothly and you have an exciting summer to look forward to.

Well, as requested here's the latest episode in the series: Big sister takes off round the world. The last time we heard from her – a postcard over three weeks ago – she was in Australia, broke and looking for work. She was in Indonesia before that and said it was brilliant. She thinks she might be able to get a job as a tour guide.

Thanks for the offer but I'm not my sister. I'm definitely going to college straight after school. I don't want my friends to get there and start the party a year before me.

That's about all for now.

Love,
Carol

## Grammar

**1** Complete each sentence with one of the words given at the end of the sentence. Two possible positions for the word are shown. Only one is correct.

1  Our quick check-in service makes ..... your journey ..... . (easier / more easily)

2  The resort seems ..... unusually ..... for this time of year. (quiet / quietly)

3  Tourist numbers have risen ..... in Spain ..... this year. (sharp / sharply)

4  You'll be staying in a ..... located ..... hotel and near to the beach.  (central / centrally)

5  We are going to arrive ..... there ....., you know. (late / lately)

6  Tourism has ..... damaged ..... the environment on the island.  (serious / seriously)

7  Fly-drive holidays to the region are ..... popular ..... . (increasing / increasingly)

8  Car hire looked ..... at first ..... but there were lots of hidden extras. (cheap / cheaply)

**2** Look up these words in a dictionary.  Find out whether the adverb form is the same as the adjective or whether the adverb form involves a spelling change. Then complete the lists below.

far  straight  happy  tragic  easy
fast  scientific  hard  incredible

| Adjectives with same adverb form | Adjectives and adverbs with a change of spelling |
|---|---|
| *late* | *simple – simply* |

**(0)** U̲N̲H̲E̲L̲P̲F̲U̲L̲   **ADVICE FOR TOURISTS**

● When travelling by train remember that it is considered (1) ..... not to help anyone who is doing a crossword puzzle.

● Comments from the public are always (2) ..... in courts of law. When you start speaking someone will shout 'Silence in court' to ensure you are heard (3) ..... .

● London barbers are (4) ..... to shave customers' armpits.

● Most foreign tourists know that they can (5) ..... take a piece of fruit, (6) ..... of charge from any open-air stall or display.

● Teenagers are not allowed upstairs on buses. If you see teenagers up there ask them (7) ..... to descend.

● On first entering an Underground train, it is (8) ..... to shake the hand of every passenger (9) ..... .

● Try the (10) ..... echo in the British Museum Reading Room.

HELP

POLITE
WELCOMING

CLEAR
DELIGHT
HAPPINESS
FREEDOM

KIND
CUSTOM
WARMTH
FAME

**3** The advice for tourists on the left appeared in an English magazine. The article intended the advice to be funny, because in each case it recommends something that is likely to get a tourist in Britain into trouble. Where there is a missing word you will need to decide whether you need an adjective or adverb form.

**exam task** Read the text on the left. Use the word given in capitals at the end of each line to form a word that fits in the space in the same line. There is an example at the beginning (0).

## Vocabulary

**1** Many activities connected with travel and tourism are described by a phrase containing the word *go*, for example, *to go camping*. Look at the words below and write down the activity you most closely associate with them using a phrase with the word *go*.

EXAMPLE:

*tents, campsites, rucksacks*
*to go camping*

1  monuments, places of interest, historical sites

2  coach, group, packed lunch

3  luggage, tickets, sun hat, books to read

4  guide, organised programme, places to stay

5  car, countryside, scenery

6  passengers, leisure deck, different ports

7  carrier bags, market, receipts

8  saddle, pedals, helmet

**2** Look at the following text. All the words missing from the text are connected with the idea of travel and tourism. Where you find a question involving a word or words that you think you have met elsewhere in this unit in the Student's Book and Workbook, look back and see if you can find it.

**exam task** Read the text below and decide which answer (**A, B, C** or **D**) best fits each space. There is an example at the beginning (**0**).

### MASS TOURISM IN THE UK

Within this generation tourism has **(0)** B. from an elite extravagance into a mass industry. **(1)** ..... tours and nose-to-tail coachloads follow the **(2)** ..... where once the solitary traveller went **(3)** ..... the Grand Tour. But many natives think that the tourist industry is destroying the very things that **(4)** ..... the tourists.

Conservation and the huge new tourist industry must learn to work together rather than against each other. Traffic can be banned in **(5)** ..... city areas as it has been in York and Cambridge. The tourist season continually **(6)** ..... so that it is becoming 'deseasonalised'. Tourists must be steered **(7)** ..... from the obvious 'honeypot' areas and **(8)** ..... to be more adventurous. Popular tourist **(9)** ....., such as the great cathedrals and colleges, are learning to provide good **(10)** ..... for mass trippers with modern information technology without letting the **(11)** ..... destroy the heritage. Natives must be educated in the importance of tourism to their **(12)** ..... .

The first historian of Britain wrote of London as a great **(13)** ..... for tourists from many nations **(14)** ..... to it by land and sea and it remains **(15)** ...... today. But in the new world of mass tourism, new techniques of managing and shepherding tourists are needed.

| | A | | B | | C | | D | |
|---|---|---|---|---|---|---|---|---|
| 0 | A | raised | B | grown | C | enlarged | D | become |
| 1 | A | luggage | B | baggage | C | package | D | parcel |
| 2 | A | routes | B | destinations | C | schedules | D | directions |
| 3 | A | around | B | on | C | off | D | about |
| 4 | A | appeal | B | want | C | attract | D | enjoy |
| 5 | A | full | B | congested | C | rushed | D | heavy |
| 6 | A | lasts | B | extends | C | reaches | D | presses |
| 7 | A | away | B | off | C | round | D | down |
| 8 | A | let | B | focused | C | encouraged | D | managed |
| 9 | A | sightseeing | B | monuments | C | interests | D | sites |
| 10 | A | reduction | B | value | C | worth | D | saving |
| 11 | A | loads | B | crowds | C | herds | D | bunches |
| 12 | A | livelihoods | B | living | C | lifetime | D | liveliness |
| 13 | A | scenery | B | recreation | C | facility | D | destination |
| 14 | A | reaching | B | arriving | C | passing | D | coming |
| 15 | A | yet | B | even | C | so | D | always |

# Preparation for speaking

**1** Look at these short exchanges between students who are discussing the pictures. Complete the question that student A asks that prompts the rest of the conversation. The first one has been done as an example.

1  A: Where do you ........*think it comes from*........?
   B: Somewhere like India.
   A: Or from south-east Asia perhaps.

2  A: Where ............................................?
   B: In America – by a holidaymaker.
   A: Yes, it could be California.

3  A: Do you ............................................?
   B: Always.
   A: Me too. I was two kilos heavier when I got back last year.

4  A: What would ............................................?
   B: Insect repellent and a mobile phone.
   A: Don't be silly. Who would you call?

5  A: How much ............................................?
   B: Probably about £200 a night.
   A: Yes, maybe more.

6  A: Why ............................................?
   B: On business probably.
   A: He wouldn't wear a suit otherwise.

7  A: How long ............................................?
   B: About two hours by car.
   A: That long?

8  A: Do you prefer ............................................?
   B: The beach.
   A: Me too. That's what makes a holiday.

**2** Find an advertisement for a holiday in English. Block out six bits of information from the advertisement, for example, details relating to the price, destination, facilities, etc. Write a question to ask another student about each piece of information you block out, e.g. Price: *How much do you think the three-day trip will cost?*

Bring your advertisement to class. Give it to another student and ask your questions to see if he or she can guess the details you have blocked out.

Birmingham
M5
Bristol

# *Exam focus* **Paper 5 Speaking**

## Part 1 Interview

**1** Think about which piece of information you might give an examiner
first in response to the following questions. Circle one of the options.

| Questions | Information |
|---|---|
| 1  Where are you from? | Ancestors  Country  Parents' birthplace  Town |
| 2  Where do you live? | Country  Town  Description  Area/suburb  Type of accommodation  Address |
| 3  What do you do? | Career plans  Qualifications  Job/studies/school  Description of job/studies |
| 4  How do you spend your holidays? | Friends/family  Type of holiday  Abroad/own country  Transport |

**2** Consider what follow-up question the examiner might ask to get
more detailed information and how you might respond. How might
a short exchange in response to each question in **1** develop?
Write each one out as a four-line dialogue.

EXAMPLE:

Examiner:  Where are you from?
You:       *I'm originally from Salzburg.*
Examiner:  *Really. So how long have you been living here?* (follow-up)
You:       *Almost three years now.* (more detail)

**3** Now look at the following examiner questions.
What would an appropriate short answer be in
each case? Remember that a short answer is a
kind of introduction to a more detailed answer
which will follow.

1  How often do you go on holiday?
2  Do you get much free time?
3  How much television do you watch?
4  What sort of music do you like?
5  Do you have plans for when you finish school?
6  How do you travel to school/work?
7  Have you lived here all your life?
8  What's the area you live in like?

Now decide how you might expand appropriately
on your answer.

**4** Here are some of the detailed answers students
gave to the questions in **3**. Think about which
question these answers are a response to and try
to fill in the missing parts.

a  'I do ..................... . I'm not that ..................... ..................
school this year, so I have most weekends
to ..................... .'

b  '..................... kinds really. It ..................... on my mood.'

c  ' ..................... of it. We moved ..................... several
years ago because of my dad's job and I think
..................... here as home.'

d  'Not really. It's a long ..................... off. I just want
to ..................... on my studies and then I'll
..................... .'

e  'It's ..................... special actually. We live in the
oldest ..................... of town with great .....................
of the harbour.'

f  ' ..................... ..................... ................. I can. I can't
..................... to go abroad more than once
..................... ..................... but I get .....................
at weekends.'

# 6 Learning

## Reading

**1** Have you ever thought of doing a summer course in the USA? What might you need to pack in your suitcase to take with you? And what attitudes would it be useful for you to have? Think about this before reading the article.

**2** Read the article to see if it mentions the same things that you thought about.

## Planning and packing for study in the USA

**0** — D

After you decide what to study and where, you need to think about what to bring to the USA. Plan carefully because if you pack more than 32 kilos or check in suitcases larger than 158cm, most international airlines will charge you high rates for overweight or oversized baggage. You may check in, free of charge, two pieces of luggage on most international flights, and you may bring two carry-on bags on board.

**1**

Students and professors dress casually on US campuses, particularly in the summer. Students wear jeans, tennis shoes, sandals, T-shirts and sometimes shorts to class.

**2**

There probably will be some occasions for more formal wear. Men will want to have a sports jacket, trousers (or a suit), shirt and tie. Women will want to have at least one smart outfit.

**3**

Should you bring any sports equipment? Certainly you will want your swimming trunks or costume. You may also want to bring your tennis racquet. Leave heavy golf clubs, bicycle, soccer balls, etc. at home. You can easily rent or borrow this equipment.

**4**

If you are going to live in a hall of residence, you may need to provide your own sheets, pillows and towels. Some schools furnish bed linen; in other schools you can purchase a service that will provide linen and also launder it. Some schools provide nothing but your bed. If you don't know what you will find, bring soap and a towel for the first night – buy anything else you need after you have settled in.

### What else to bring

**5**

Some things you need to bring to the USA won't be packed in a suitcase – they will be packed in your mind. Your expectations and attitudes can make a difference to how you enjoy your summer in the USA.

**6**

North American people value individual experience. Be prepared to be independent!

**7**

You will miss home, family and friends at first. This will be temporary until you meet new friends and become familiar with your new environment.

**8**

You will also want to bring special attitudes. These include a readiness to reach out to strangers for friendship and to ask for directions or assistance if you need them.

**9**

Have a good trip, and enjoy your educational adventure.

**3** **exam task** Choose the most suitable heading from the list **A–K** for each part (1–9) of the article. There is one extra heading which you do not need to use. There is an example at the beginning (0).

A Missing and meeting people
B Essential items
C Be yourself
D Luggage
E Leisure items
F All the best

G Daily dress
H Attitudes
I The right frame of mind
J Bedding
K Formal dress

**4** Here are drawings of items mentioned in the article. Label them.

a

b

c

d

e

f

g

h

i

j

k

**5** Imagine some students are coming from a foreign country to spend a term in your school. Write a list including everything they would need to bring with them (these may be items, knowledge or attitudes).

Then write a letter or design a leaflet advising foreign students what to bring and why.

# Writing

**1** Here is a letter written by a student after their first day in a foreign country. Read it to see if their first impressions are positive or negative. How would you feel in the same situations?

Dear all,

Well, you asked me to write as soon as I got here, so here I am — not quite punctual, but not bad — only a few hours late. First of all, let me tell you that I'm fine and all is well, so you have nothing to worry about. Now let me tell you about my adventures to date. Well, the flight from Athens (1)….. (to be) OK. In some ways it was very long and pretty boring — I (2) ….. (not manage) to sleep, and I didn't watch the film as it was all in French so I (3) ….. (can not) understand most of it, but there was this great guy sitting next to me who (4) …..(tell) me all about his job — he (5) ….. (work) as a helicopter engineer and travels all over the world doing exciting things. I also (6)….. (get) to see some exciting things from the plane — the Alps with snow on them, the Eiffel Tower in Paris and the River Thames as we flew in to London.

When we got here I was met at the airport — just as the school rep.(7) …..(arrange). It all went very smoothly, and we (8)….. (travel) up here by coach. Then I met my host family, who (9)….. (seem) really nice, and after that I was shown my room. You should see it! It (10) ….. (be) fabulous. I've got my own TV and sound system, a supply of CDs, a computer with the Internet, and a kettle and things for me to make hot drinks. It's so great I (11)…..(not go) out since.

Anyway, it's getting late now, so I'll say bye-bye.

Love to you all. I hope you're all fine.

**2** This letter is a mixture of a narrative and a description of a present situation. Put the verbs in brackets into the right tense.

**3** Much of the language in this letter is informal because it is a letter written to close friends or family. Underline the informal language.

**4** Why are there just two main paragraphs in this letter?

**5** **exam task** Write a letter in **120–180** words to a friend of yours describing your first impressions of a summer course you went on recently. The course can be real or imaginary, enjoyable or boring, etc.

# Grammar

**1** Here is part of a letter from a school to parents about a school camp.
Read it and decide whether you would like to go on this camp.

Dear Parents,

## Autumn School Camp

This year's autumn camp will take place from Wednesday October 7th to Friday October 9th inclusive. The camp is for Year 9 students.

**Setting**  The Miranda Camp is **(1)** ..... in the Vose Park at Marton. It is an outdoor recreational centre which **(2)** ..... the opportunity to enjoy outdoor life.

**Activities**  The students will **(3)** ..... in a programme of challenging outdoor activities including orienteering, canoeing, rock climbing, sailing and general sporting activities. It is **(4)** ..... that such activities provide a challenge and stimulus not found in the classroom and **(5)** ..... they have an important role to play in the education of the whole child. The community life of the camp also **(6)** ..... the opportunity for students to develop their sense of self-discipline, cooperation, friendship and mutual understanding.

**Facilities**  The camp has seven well-equipped houses. Organised activities **(7)** ..... archery, rope climbing and roller skating. There are also squash, badminton and table tennis facilities. The swimming pool **(8)** ..... also be open. Catering is provided by the canteen.

**Accommodation**  The air-conditioned dormitories accommodate eight people and are on two floors. There are hot showers on **(9)** ..... floors. Bedding is provided.

**Staff**  The students will be accompanied by 11 members of staff **(10)** ..... the whole stay.

**Cost**  The cost of the camp **(11)** ..... transport, board and lodging will be £100. Cheques should be crossed and made payable **(12)** ..... Miranda College.

**2** **exam task** Now read the letter again and think of the word which best fits each space. Use only one word in each space.

**3** Put a tick (✓) by the activities you have done, and a cross (✗) by those you have never done.

| orienteering | rock climbing | canoeing | sailing |
| rope climbing | roller skating | table tennis | swimming |

In Unit 6 of the Student's Book you studied the present perfect tense and some prepositions of time. Use these structures to write sentences about yourself and the activities above like this:

- I have never ...
- I ... since/for ...
- I went ... *ing* in/on/during/at ...
- I have always/never wanted to ... because ...

## Vocabulary

**1** Read this article about a true story.
Do you agree with the punishment given to the girl?

**2** **exam task** Read the article again and decide which answer **A**, **B**, **C** or **D** best fits each space.
There is an example at the beginning **(0)**.

**3** List all the words in the article that are related to school.

| 0 | **A** taken | **B** arrested | **C** captured | **D** sentenced |
|---|---|---|---|---|
| 1 | **A** at | **B** against | **C** off | **D** across |
| 2 | **A** clothing | **B** wearing | **C** putting | **D** dressing |
| 3 | **A** attend | **B** see | **C** meet | **D** face |
| 4 | **A** worrying | **B** sad | **C** upset | **D** challenging |
| 5 | **A** took | **B** grabbed | **C** hit | **D** touched |
| 6 | **A** while | **B** unless | **C** provided | **D** until |
| 7 | **A** let | **B** allowed | **C** released | **D** sent |
| 8 | **A** in | **B** back | **C** again | **D** by |
| 9 | **A** sent | **B** excluded | **C** suspended | **D** expelled |

### SCHOOLGIRL ARRESTED FOR HITTING TEACHER

A 14-year-old schoolgirl was **(0)** B̲. for allegedly assaulting a woman teacher yesterday after an argument at her secondary school over her uniform. The third year student clashed with her teacher after being told **(1)** ..... for arriving at morning assembly **(2)** ..... a black jacket and earrings and with a mobile phone in her hand.

She was taken to **(3)** ..... the head who asked her to leave her jacket and earrings and phone and collect them after school. At that, she became **(4)** ..... and ran out of the office.

The head said she then ran to her classroom but met her teacher on the stairs. 'The schoolgirl **(5)** ..... the teacher's jacket collar and punched her in the chest,' he said. She held on to the teacher **(6)** ..... she was told the police would be called.

She was taken to a police station and later **(7)** ..... on bail of £250 and told to report **(8)** ..... on February 25. The girl has been **(9)** ..... from school for three days.

## Preparation for speaking

Here are two photos of quite different language classrooms. List the vocabulary and expressions of comparison and contrast that you could use to compare and contrast them. Practise comparing and contrasting them, in your head or out loud.

# Exam focus  Paper 1 Reading

## Part 4 Multiple matching

**exam task** You are going to read a magazine article in which people recall their favourite teachers. For questions 1–8, choose from texts **A–D**. Texts may be chosen more than once. When more than one answer is required these may be given in any order.

### Which teacher or teachers

taught young children? | 1 |

showed great enthusiasm for their subject? | 2 | |

had a sense of humour? | 3 | |

brought out the best in each student? | 4 | |

inspired students' interest in their subject? | 5 | | |

obviously thought carefully about the content of their lessons? | 6 |

gave the students a sense of self-esteem? | 7 | |

was very good at telling a story? | 8 |

### A

When I think back to all the teachers I had at school one stands out clearly. She was my history teacher. She had this wonderful way of making history live. When she spoke about it, it became a dramatic story that had us sitting on the edge of our chairs in excitement.

### B

The best teacher I've ever had was an English teacher. He was extremely professional in his approach. He always came to class with his lesson well prepared and full of ideas that he knew would appeal to us. But he also had this talent for being able to combine professionalism with a great sense of humour that had us constantly laughing as well as cracking jokes ourselves. Yet all the time he kept up the pressure, and kept us working. We loved his lessons.

### C

The teacher I most appreciate is one who was able to see the potential in me and worked patiently with me to realise that potential. He turned me from a shy, somewhat unenthusiastic student into a confident and keen actor. He did this through his sensitivity to individuals, his patience with, belief in and insight into each and every student, and his passion for acting.

### D

My best teacher was my very first teacher. I remember her clearly to this day. Her name was Mrs Cooke. She was kind, gentle, encouraging, funny, firm and inspiring. I think she taught us to value calmness and a sense of direction, ourselves and one another.

# Places

## Reading

**1** The letters in the following words have all been jumbled. Sort the letters out to make words. Each word is the name of a type of natural disaster.

EXAMPLE:

**dalitvwae** *tidal wave*

| ofldo | urhirncae |
|---|---|
| lavchnaea | liolispl |
| rodutgh | eaquthkae |
| lpageu | orstefrefi |

**2** Sometimes in a text you will meet words that you do not immediately recognise. You may be able to work out what they mean, however, by using other information in the text.

Some of the words and phrases in the text have been highlighted. Answer the questions about these words and then guess the meaning of the word. Check the word in a dictionary to see if you were right.

## The Rainmaker

**0**                               (

American Indians have long been famous for the practice of rain-dancing. The most well-known American rainmaker of modern times, however, was not an American Indian but Charles Hatfield, who claimed he could make it pour by using far more scientific methods.

**1**

Hatfield was a professional rainmaker. For more than 30 years, he offered his services to those in need of water – saving crops, breaking droughts and filling lakes. He offered to rid London of its smogs and to water the Sahara.

**2**

Hatfield's most remarkable achievement, however, was reserved for California. In December 1915, in return for a payment of $10,000, he volunteered to fill the huge reservoir at Morena Dam, which supplied water to San Diego.

**3**

The reservoir could hold 15 billion gallons of water but, since its construction, had never been more than one-third full. So confident was Hatfield of success that he came up with the terms: no rain, no pay.

**4**

The San Diego City Council accepted his offer and, on 1 January 1916, Hatfield started erecting a wooden tower on the top of which he placed large galvanizing trays containing his secret moisture-attracting substance.

**5**

Within four days it was raining. On 10 January, it began to pour with rain – and it did not stop for 10 days. Hatfield's popularity was on the wane as streets flooded, highways closed and phone lines were cut off. Rivers overflowed, washing away 200 bridges, and houses were demolished by a 12m high wall of water when the nearby Lower Otay Dam crumbled. Fifty people lost their lives.

**6**

A brief respite was followed by yet more downpours so that by 26 January, the water level at the Morena dam was rising by ½ metre an hour. It finally came to a halt just 12cm from the top of the dam, thus averting a disaster of calamitous proportions.

**7**

Hatfield considered that he had fulfilled his part of the bargain. The Council, however, flatly refused to pay him, insisting that the deluge was an act of God.

**a** What is this most likely to be: people, animals or plants?

**b** What word in the next paragraph tells you this is man-made?

**c** How does the punctuation help us to work out the meaning of this word?

**d** What is he doing: building or knocking something down?

**e** What was probably happening to his popularity?

**f** What are the two parts of this word?

**g** Causing or preventing?

**h** What previous information in the text does this word refer to?

**3** **exam task** Choose the most suitable heading from the list (A–I) for each part (1–7) of the text. There is one extra heading which you do not need to use. There is an example at the beginning (0).

A  The tragic cost of rain

B  Method or madness

C  An easy offer to accept

D  Very different views

E  Thinking on a large scale

F  Dying of thirst

G  A very close thing

H  His finest moment

I  A native tradition

**4** The text mentions several problems that the heavy rains caused. Look at the things on the left, which were mentioned in the text. Without looking back at the text, match these things to one of the verbs on the right describing the problems caused.

| | |
|---|---|
| phone lines | overflowed |
| houses | flooded |
| rivers | were washed away |
| bridges | were cut off |
| lives | crumbled |
| streets | closed |
| highways | were lost |
| a dam | were demolished |

Now look back at the text and see if you were right.

**5** Find out about a famous natural disaster. From the information or article you find, write down the headline or make one up for the disaster, e.g.

Krakatoa erupts    Hurricane Mitch hits

Under your headline write a matching exercise like the one in **4** with words from the article describing what damage was caused. Bring your exercise to class for other students to do.

## Writing

**1** The text below is a description of a walk. Underline examples of the following structures which are all commonly used in descriptions:

a  a verb of the senses followed by *-ing*

b  relative clauses beginning with 'where'

c  the past perfect used to explain why something looked the way it did

d  an example of a participle clause

I walked through old woods where the light was soft, the air cool. Where the trees parted or had been burned by arsonists there were wild flowers, butterflies, basking lizards, scents rising as my body brushed against herbs and plants. The path itself, climbing up to 2,500 ft, was ancient. Not a Roman road, mind you. It was older and more primitive than that, narrow in places, slippery in others. Above all, it was empty. I met three people on the way and in that solitude, with no noise from traffic, neighbours or road menders, my senses came alive and I started to hear birdsong, leaves falling, the call of a farmer further down the slope, the slither of a lizard or snake.

**2** Now write a description of a favourite walk or place that you know. Use the following outline, based on the text above, to help you.

I walked towards … where …

There was/were … where …

The path itself …

There was no …

I could hear/see …

It felt …

## Grammar

**1** Read this story about a real-life rescue by city firemen in the USA. Think carefully about the time sequence of events and put the verbs in brackets into the correct form. All verbs in the simple past form have been left in, verbs in other forms have not.

**2** Read this 'impression' poem, and notice the use of the gerund structure.

---

### At the Bus Stop

*Watches slowly ticking*
*Leaves blowing by*
*People gazing in the distance*
*Shuffling in the queue*

*Waiting for a lifetime*
*Journeys starting late*
*Hoping this is it*
*Number 68 going past*

---

Now write your own impression poem called 'Block of Flats'. Use the gerund form and mix different sights, thoughts, sounds, feelings, etc.

# Trapped in a burning elevator

**9.10 am**   Above him, the sounds of workers (1) ...................... (run) across the third floor echoed down the shaft into the elevator. 'There's a fire,' someone screamed. Then he heard Semone's voice: 'Everybody out of the building.' 'Hey, I'm stuck in the elevator,' Dylan yelled as loud as he could.

**9.17 am**   Fire inspector Gary Boyles was already at the warehouse where a fire (2) ...................... (rage) in a builder's skip. He approached a group of employees gathered in a parking lot. Al Semone (3) ...................... (count) heads. Suddenly he asked, 'Where's Dylan?' Before anyone could answer, he and Boyles (4) ...................... (run) back into the building.

**9.20 am**   (5) ...................... (look) out of a window, Boyles saw fire (6) ...................... (climb) up the building, (7) ...................... (use) the plastic chute as a route to the upper floors. Down below, the fire trucks (8) ...................... (arrive) and Boyles yelled: 'There's a guy stuck in an elevator on the second floor.'

**9.30 am**   The building (9) ...................... (begin) to give way. Chunks of hot concrete dropped down the shaft into the elevator. Dylan looked up and saw flames (10) ...................... (shoot) through the crack in the elevator doors, (11) ...................... (threaten) to ignite the paper inside.

**9.38 am**   (12) ...................... (monitor) the fire from their command vehicle, two fire officials looked at their watches. The warehouse (13) ...................... (burn) for about 20 minutes and the top floors were completely engulfed. Experience (14) ...................... (teach) them that now was the time when the upper levels (15) ...................... (collapse). All trucks were ordered to blow their horns, (16) ...................... (sound) the warning to clear the building. Two minutes later a fire captain called in on the radio: 'We have a person trapped in an elevator. Squad One is trying to effect a rescue.'

**9.46 am**   Dylan (17) ...................... (hear) the order to clear the building. They (18) ...................... (go) to leave him, he thought.

**9.48 am**   Firemen Beahm and Thompson found a stairwell (19) ...................... (lead) to the basement. Beahm eyed a two-inch pipe, (20) ...................... (come) out of the wall. 'This has to be it,' he said. He beat on the pipe with his axe until he (21) ...................... (flatten) his blade. A stream of fluid spurted out.

**9.53 am**   Dylan felt the elevator lurch. He scooted round so his feet were in front of the door. When he felt a strong pair of hands on his legs, he leapt from the elevator. He was rushed to an ambulance. Semone (22) ...................... (wait) inside. 'Glad to see you,' he said. On the way to the hospital Dylan cried quietly, not (23) ...................... (believe) he (24) ...................... (survive).

**3** exam task For questions 1–15, read the text below and think of the word which best fits each space. Use only one word in each space. There is an example at the beginning (0).

## Italy through the year

Throughout Italy, **(0)** the... variety of local character and colour is astonishing. This is mainly due **(1)** ..... the survival of regionalism, particularly **(2)** ..... the southern parts of the country. Old traditions, customs and lifestyles are still greatly respected and **(3)** ..... is a deep attachment to the land, **(4)** ..... is reflected in the healthy interest in the food and produce, as **(5)** ..... as the celebration of seasonal religious and secular events. Annual festivals, whether in rural **(6)** ..... urban areas, range from wine-tasting and gastronomic celebrations **(7)** ..... elaborate commemorations of **(8)** ..... single patron saint imaginable.

The Italian peninsula has **(9)** ..... varied climate falling into three **(10)** ..... distinct geographical regions. Cold Alpine winters and warm, wet summers characterise **(11)** ..... northern regions. In the extensive Po Valley, arid summers contrast **(12)** ..... freezing, damp winters. The rest of Italy has a pleasant climate **(13)** ..... long hot summers and mild winters. Cooler **(14)** ..... along the backbone of the Appenines can bring snow **(15)** ..... the winter months.

*Map shows ITALY with Milan, Turin, Genoa, ROME, Naples.*

# Vocabulary

**1** exam task For questions 1–12, read the text below. Use the word given in capitals at the end of each line to form a word that fits in the space in the same line. There is an example at the beginning (0).

### GRAND STAIRCASE-ESCALANTE
#### The USA's newest national monument

| | |
|---|---|
| From the high ground, try to take it all in, 1.7 million desolate, **(0)** thrilling.. | THRILL |
| acres. The landscape is so **(1)** ..... vast, you might need two pairs of | POSSIBLE |
| binoculars. These **(2)** ....., this primitiveness, should have crushed the | DISTANT |
| Mormon **(3)** ..... . But didn't. Their 119-year-old wagon-wheel | SETTLE |
| ruts still snake alongside Hole-in-the-Rock Road. | |
| | |
| Grand Staircase-Escalante hasn't the fame of the **(4)** ..... parks | NATION |
| that surround it. Yet it defines **(5)** ..... notions of the Old West. | ROMANCE |
| The region is so remote that it was the last area to be **(6)** ..... in | MAP |
| the lower 48 states. Mail **(7)** ..... was made by mule into the 1930s. | DELIVER |
| It is so fragile that a single **(8)** ..... can wipe out decades of | FOOT |
| **(9)** ..... of the crust holding the desert floor together. | GROW |
| The **(10)** ..... of roads in the interior are mostly rutted and unpaved | HAND |
| and often **(11)** ..... . A large part of the area probably looks much | PASS |
| the same as it did when the Anasazi were the only **(12)** ..... | INHABIT |
| 900 years ago. And many feel that's the way it should remain. | |

**2** exam task For questions 1–15, read the text below and decide which answer A, B, C or D best fits each space. There is an example at the beginning (0).

## Red River Rising

As the (0) ..D. sun turned its warming (1) ..... on the frigid (2) ....., it set in motion a deadly chain of (3) ..... . The snow and ice of the long, cold winter (4) ..... into water that fed and swelled the Red River, which forms on the North Dakota–Minnesota (5) ..... . The river grew and spread, swallowing everything in its (6) ..... .

The water rose with such speed that some people (7) ..... their vehicles in the street and escaped (8) ..... city dump trucks. Hospitals and nursing homes were (9) ..... . Family members were scattered, (10) ..... refuge in shelters (11) ..... North Dakota and Minnesota.

(12) ..... downtown Grand Forks under five feet of water and more than 40,000 people (13) ....., there (14) ..... to be but one mild consolation: things could not possibly (15) ..... any worse.

| 0 | A season | B cold | C wintry | D spring |
|---|---|---|---|---|
| 1 | A lights | B rays | C sunsets | D lines |
| 2 | A landscape | B view | C space | D scenery |
| 3 | A causes | B effects | C events | D occasions |
| 4 | A heated | B dripped | C melted | D washed |
| 5 | A valley | B countryside | C region | D border |
| 6 | A path | B passage | C route | D slope |
| 7 | A neglected | B ignored | C abandoned | D forgot |
| 8 | A boarding | B aboard | C boarded | D abroad |
| 9 | A disappeared | B departed | C emptied | D exited |
| 10 | A having | B knowing | C finding | D waiting |
| 11 | A through | B across | C among | D together |
| 12 | A As | B Like | C With | D From |
| 13 | A lonely | B survived | C deserted | D homeless |
| 14 | A used | B seemed | C had | D found |
| 15 | A turn | B develop | C get | D come |

# Preparation for speaking

**1** Look at these answers to questions about getting to and from places. What were the questions?

1 .......................................................? Sure, I'm going your way anyway.

2 .......................................................? About two hours by car.

3 .......................................................? I walked all the way.

4 .......................................................? Traffic was bad.

5 .......................................................? No, the nearest garage is in town.

6 .......................................................? No, there's no airport.

7 .......................................................? All right, let's go somewhere different.

8 .......................................................? Yes, but it's worth it for the scenery.

9 .......................................................? No, Joe came with me in the car.

10 .......................................................? They run until about midnight.

**2** Look at these six different urban problems. Think about the largest city in your country and put the problems in order of importance: most serious to least serious.

> Pollution   Rubbish collection
> Overcrowding   Homeless people
> Traffic congestion   Street crime

Note down a few ideas about why each one is more important or less important than the others. In class you will be asked to defend your views.

# Exam focus  Paper 2 Writing

## Part 2 Writing a story

**1** Look at this student's story. The student's task was to write a story for
a school magazine about a real or imaginary embarrassing incident,
ending with the words: *I've never felt so stupid in my life.* There are
10 mistakes in the story connected with the use of tenses, participles
and relative clauses. Find and correct these mistakes.

It was Friday after school and as usual I was sitting at a plastic table
surrounding by styrofoam cups and the remains of burgers. My friends just left
and I was alone.

a) ⋆ ⋆ ⋆

A woman which had sat at the next table got up and left carrying her young
child in her arms. I just finished my drink when I noticed a black leather
handbag on the floor behind the chair where the woman was with her child.

b) ⋆ ⋆ ⋆

I picked up the bag and rushed downstairs. The woman obviously already left
the café so I went outside and saw her to push her child in a pram on the other
side of the road. I was just about to call out when a large hand was grabbing
my shoulder. 'Hey, that's my wife's bag,' said a red-faced giant. He snatched
the bag from my trembling hands and before I explained, slapped me on the
ear and went back inside. I can honestly say I've never felt so stupid in my life.

**2** There are two gaps in the story. Complete the story like this:
   **a** Describe what is going on in the café and explain why you are alone.
   **b** Describe the thoughts which eventually make you take the bag and
   run downstairs.

**3** **exam task** Your class teacher has asked for real or imaginary stories to
include in a student magazine, ending with the words:
*It was the worst night I have ever spent anywhere.*
Your story should be between **120–180** words.

## Reading

**1** Most big bands employ 'roadies' to help them with their equipment. Look at this picture. What do you think the roadies might do to get the show ready?

**2** **exam task** You are going to read a text about the job of a 'band roadie'. Seven sentences have been removed from the text. Choose from the sentences A–H the one which fits each gap. There is one extra sentence which you do not need to use. There is an example at the beginning (0).

**A** Skills in handling the equipment are picked up along the way.

**B** It's also up to the employer to decide whether you are worth the money you are asking.

**C** They may need to do jobs and solve problems they've never tackled before.

**D** When the band is on the road there may be a travelling crew of 14.

**E** But when there is a panic on, everyone will do what has to be done.

**F** Your salary depends on the success of the band.

**G** Roadies begin by helping out friends who belong to a pop group.

**H** Stage absence means he has done his groundwork properly.

---

# BAND ROADIE

While the ideal rock star has a charismatic stage presence, the ideal roadie is one who is never seen. **0** [H] – though he may stand worrying out of sight during a concert in case anything goes wrong with the equipment. When everything is set up and ready to go, and there are 50,000 or so people in the audience, there can be 'quite a buzz' when the band hits the stage – and everything works right. **1** [ ] They load their amplifier and drums and so forth into the hired van, and set it all up on stage for local gigs. Then they'll have the experience that they'll be asked about when they go for interviews. The next stage is working in a loading crew working locally, doing the donkey work. **2** [ ] Some roadies specialise with guitars and amps, others on drums or synthesisers. Others specialise in lighting, sound or 'rigging' (hanging stuff from the roof), as stage managers or as floor managers. **3** [ ] Bands are varied in the equipment that they use. Some need roadies for recording and rehearsal times; others only during a tour. **4** [ ] This includes four to deal with lighting, four sound people to set up the 'black boxes', one rigger, two in charge of the van gear, stage manager and two catering people. They live in the sleeper bus, but not much; hours can run from 7am to 2am. Living on a bus with 13 other people for a month is like living in a (comfortable) submarine, so any arguments have to be sorted out speedily.

Those who are lucky, who are good workers and understand the equipment, can eventually work for 52 weeks of the year, though they need perseverance and must be prepared to spend time sitting around twiddling their thumbs waiting for the next job. **5** [ ] Roadies doing the same job but with different bands may be getting twice as much – or half as much – as one another. **6** [ ] It's a high pressure world, complex and unique, but away from the 9 to 5 routines, which is why people like it. You can find yourself in some very strange places in the world, sometimes having to adapt accordingly.

---

**3** Read the text again and write the following list.

**Skills and experience required by a roadie**

- 
- 
- 
- 
- 
- 

**4** **exam task** These sentences are based on the text. Complete the second sentence so that it has a similar meaning to the first sentence, using the word given. Do not change the word given. You must use between two and five words, including the word given.

1 Skills in handling the equipment are picked up along the way.
Roadies learn ......................................... along the way. **how**

2 When there is a panic on, everyone will do what is necessary.
When there is a panic on, everyone will do ......................................... done. **needs**

3 Bands differ in the kind of equipment that they use.
What equipment is used ......................................... band. **varies**

4 Any arguments have to be sorted out speedily.
You ......................................... arguments speedily. **need**

5 Your salary depends on the success of the band.
How ......................................... the success of the band. **much**

6 It's up to the employer to decide your salary.
It's ......................................... salary. **who**

7 The job doesn't involve regular hours, which is why people like it.
The ......................................... job is because it doesn't involve regular hours. **reason**

# Writing

## Narratives

**1** Some strange things can happen in all kinds of jobs. Read this jumbled text to find out what happened to a nanny and the baby she was looking after.

---

**A**

The driver discovered the non-paying passenger when his next passenger swung open the back door to find the seat already occupied.

**B**

The nanny called the police, and taxi operators in turn put drivers on the lookout.

**C**

But Max was sleeping so peacefully, the 30-year-old driver did not know he was there until he stopped for another passenger.

**D**

The baby, whose name is Max, was being taken by his New Zealand nanny to visit his mother, a lawyer in a large bank, for an afternoon feed.

**E**

He drove to a local police station where a woman police officer took care of Max until he was reunited with his parents, an hour after he began his solo adventure.

**F**

A nanny left a cab driver with more than a tip yesterday when the taxi drove off with a six-month-old baby sleeping on the back seat.

**G**

The nanny got out of the cab and took the baby's pushchair out of the boot, only to see the vehicle zip off in search of a new passenger.

---

**2** When we write we use lots of linking devices to join sentences and paragraphs. Use these to work out the correct sequence of paragraphs for this story.

**3** Underline the words in the text which show the sequence of events.

**4** Only two tenses are used in this narrative. What are they? Underline all examples of one, and circle all examples of the other. Why does the writer sometimes use one tense and sometimes the other?

**5** What would you have done at the end of the story if you had been:
the nanny, the taxi driver, the baby's parents or the baby(!)?

**6** **exam task** You have decided to enter a short story competition. The competition rules say that the story must begin like this:

*Another morning, another newspaper, another search through the job ads for a summer job. I was getting depressed and desperate – would I ever be able to earn some extra money? I was just about to throw the paper in the bin when suddenly a tiny ad caught my eye. It looked like the answer to my dreams.*

In **120–180** words write the story for the competition.

## Grammar

**1** In some countries, people applying for jobs write a CV (curriculum vitae) which is a summary of their abilities, qualifications and relevant experience. Do people in your country write CVs? How might they be useful for job applications?

**2** Here is the first part of some advice on how to write a CV. Complete the blanks with *a/an*, *the* or – (nothing).

### The Perfect CV in Just Ten Steps

**Here, compressed into a ten-point plan, is our advice on how to write a perfect CV.**

1  Keep it short, no more than (1) ............... three pages. Any longer and it will not be read. Too short and you leave your reader guessing.

2  Start with your personal details, but don't include names and ages of your children, nor every exam you passed and (2) ............... school you attended. Keep this short, include all your contact details and do not use more than half (3) ............... page.

3  Please, no personal introduction describing with (4) ............... lots of adjectives how wonderful you are. (5) ............... experienced recruiter never reads it – *they* are the ones who are expected to assess your ability, not you.

4  Put your current job first – reverse chronology throughout. What you are doing is what counts, not where you started.

5  We want to see your current organisation's or company's name and your job together with (6) ............... relevant dates. Use (7) ............... nice bold heading, and always remember that (8) ............... upper and lower-case headings are much easier to read than EVERYTHING IN (9) ............... CAPITALS.

**3** exam task  Here is the rest of the advice on how to write a CV. Look carefully at each line. Some of the lines are correct and some have a word which should not be there. If a line is correct, put a tick (✓) by it. If a line has a word which should not be there, write the word beside the line. There is an example at the beginning (0).

### The Perfect CV in Just the Ten Steps (continued)

0    Just the Ten Steps (continued)    the

1  6  Make it easy for the reader to pick out
2     your success in each the job. So have a
3     heading 'Major Achievements' followed
4     by no fewer than three, and no more
5     than six bullet points which succinctly
6     outlining your triumphs.

7  7  A few sentences after the bullet points
8     should to explain in more detail the role
9     you play in your organisation and the
10    context in which you work.

11  8  Repeat the same format for previous
12     jobs, but you make each progressively
14     more shorter, as your earlier jobs usually
13     involve less responsibility.

15  9  By all means include extra-curricular or
16     the other interesting personal activities,
17     but let us to see them at the end of the
18     CV, not in other sections.

19  10  You may (briefly) outline the type of
20     challenge what you are looking for, and
21     explain why you want it, but do to keep
22     it short and to the point.

So there you are.
Good luck with your job hunting.

## Vocabulary

**1** **exam task** Use the word given in capitals at the end of each line to form a word that fits in the space in the same line. There is an example at the beginning (0).

---

*Leaving school?*

### Become an ASSISTANT MANAGER

You will start with (0) .approximately. six months' (1) ....., consisting of on-the-job experience and several classroom sessions. Once you have (2) ..... this, you should be a (3) ..... and capable employee who is ready to take on full assistant manager (4) ..... .

After this, your Store (5) ..... will continue to train you. You will increase your confidence and (6) ..... by experiencing the everyday (7) ..... of a store and being challenged by a fast-moving and (8) ..... employer. You will need to assist in maximising store profits through loss prevention, customer (9) ....., budget control, the (10) ..... of staff, etc.

APPROXIMATE
TRAIN

COMPLETE
CONFIDENCE

RESPONSIBLE

SUPERVISE

ABLE
RUN
DEMAND

SERVE
RECRUIT

---

**2** Can you think of a job beginning with each of these letters?
A, B, C, D, F, L, N, P, S, T.

## Preparation for speaking

Collect some job-related photos from magazines or newspapers. Label eight job-related items in the photos and check their word stress in a dictionary. Prepare to compare and contrast your photos. Look at the Language boxes in the Speaking sections of the Student's Book to help you prepare. Be ready to talk about your photos in class.

# Exam focus  Paper 3 Use of English

## Part 3 'Key' word-transformation and Part 5 Word formation

**1** **exam task** Complete the second sentence so that it has a similar meaning to the first sentence, using the word given. Do not change the word given. You must use between two and five words, including the word given.

1  I haven't received the application form yet.
They ........................................... the application form.          **still**

2  His boss sacked him about two weeks ago.
He ........................................... about two weeks ago.          **fired**

3  I'd love them to give me a pay rise.
I ........................................... a pay rise.          **wish**

4  It didn't matter that they didn't promote me.
I ........................................... promoted.          **mind**

5  It was really difficult for her to find another job.
She ........................................... another job.          **difficulty**

6  He has worked for his sister for the last ten years.
He ........................................... his sister for the last ten years.          **employed**

7  What I really want to do is become a top surgeon.
My ........................................... a top surgeon.          **ambition**

**2** **exam task** Read the text below. Use the word given in capitals at the end of each line to form a word that fits in the space in the same line.

### LEARN YOUR JOB SKILLS FROM YOUR TEACHER

A teacher standing at the front of a History class is seldom teaching history alone. A good teacher is also **(1)** ..... self-expression, management ability, **(2)** ..... skills, and a whole host of other skills that may be **(3)** ..... for you later in life. There are certain basic **(4)** ..... that everyone needs to have if they are to be **(5)** ..... in education, employment and even in social circumstances. Learning these skills is **(6)** ..... important at secondary school level, in order to **(7)** ..... prepare for further education or the **(8)** ..... world. A minimum level of **(9)** ..... is demanded by all employers, colleges and universities. The more **(10)** ..... you are in those areas the more the **(11)** ..... believes you will be competent.

These personal **(12)** ..... skills differ from other school subjects in that they cannot be taught in **(13)** ..... from the rest of the school curriculum.

**DEMONSTRATE**
**COMMUNICATE**
**USE**
**ABLE**
**SUCCESS**

**SPECIAL**
**FULL**
**WORK**
**COMPETENT**
**ADVANCE**
**ORGANISE**

**DEVELOP**
**ISOLATE**

# **9** Shopping and services

## *Reading*

**1** Match a word in the first list with a word in the second list.

> compact   shopping   pet   carrier   shop
> check   lip   shop   bum   wishing

> complex   assistant   out   shop   well
> bag   disc   stick   lifting   bag

Which of the words you have made are written as one word and which as two separate words? Check your answers in the text (and note that one of them is in a different form).

**2** **exam task** Set yourself a time limit of 15 minutes to do this task. You are going to read six letters written by teenagers to a magazine.

For questions 1–14, choose from the letters **A–F**. When more than one answer is required, these may be given in any order. There is an example at the beginning **(0)**.

In which letter are the following mentioned?

| | | | |
|---|---|---|---|
| Something you keep money in | 0 C | 1 | |
| Getting wet | 2 | | |
| Committing a crime | 3 | | |
| Getting money back from a shop | 4 | | |
| Contacting a shop before you go | 5 | | |
| A misunderstanding | 6 | 7 | 8 |
| A place where you pay in shops | 9 | 10 | 11 |
| A present | 12 | 13 | |
| Replacing damaged goods | 14 | | |

## Our shopping disasters

*Teenagers write in with their shopping horror stories*

**A**

My mum and I were in Berwick shopping and when we were going past Boots I saw this big sign above the CDs that said 'Free.' So I went in and took one. When I came out my mum was horrified and asked what I thought I was doing shoplifting like that. I told her about the sign and she pointed out that in small letters underneath it had said 'when you buy a lipstick'. I felt so stupid, especially when mum made me take it back to the shop.

**B**

I'd always wanted a hamster, so I was really excited when Dad ordered me one from the pet shop. When we went to pick it up the assistant at the counter said 'name' and straight away I said 'Cuddles'. It wasn't until I saw him give me a funny look that I realised he wanted our surname for collection, not the hamster's name.

**C**

When I was younger I went to a big shopping complex with my mum. When she wasn't looking I took all my birthday money out of my bumbag and threw it in the wishing well. When my mum realised what I had done she made me take off my shoes and socks and wade in to pick up all the pound coins. Everyone was staring at me and I was bright red.

**3** **exam task** Choose the most suitable heading from the list **1–7** for each of the letters **A–F**. There is one extra heading which you do not need to use.

1  Here to pick it up
2  Not such a special offer
3  Punishment in public
4  Feeling silly a second time
5  Too much of a hurry
6  Knowing the brand
7  Changing your mind

---

| **D** |

Once I bought a pair of trousers but when I tried them on at home I realised they were too big so I put them on the chair in my room. The next day I decided to take them back and grabbed them from the chair and put them back in the carrier bag. At the shop I went up to the counter to ask for a refund but when the lady pulled them out, they were a pair I'd had for over two years. I'd picked up the wrong ones at home. I just grabbed them and ran red-faced out of the shop.

| **E** |

One day my mother asked me to go to the shops for her and gave me a list. One of the things mentioned was Big Soup so I took home a huge tin of tomato soup but when I handed it to my mum she started laughing. It turns out the actual name of the soup was Big Soup and she made me go back and change it.

| **F** |

Something really embarrassing happened to me in a local shop. I had to get some groceries for my mum and went in on my rollerblades. When I went to pay, I slid and dropped a box of eggs – two of them broke and the rest went rolling everywhere. A shop assistant cleared up the mess and got another box. That was bad enough but when it was my turn at the checkout again I realised I'd come out without my purse.

---

**4** A number of phrasal verbs are used in the letters in the text in **2**. Look at the dictionary entries for these words from the *Cambridge International Dictionary of English*. Complete the dictionary entries with verbs used in the letters.

Where there is more than one entry or example for a verb this means that in the letters opposite there are examples of different meanings of the same phrasal verb.

1  .................... *obj* [COLLECT] to collect or to go and get • *When you're in town could you* .................... **up** *the books I ordered?*

.................... *obj* [REMOVE] *v* to remove or move (something) with your fingers or hands • *He* .................... **up** (= lifted) *his suitcase and moved it away from the door* • *A group of us went out to* .................... **up** (= lift and remove) *the litter left on the grass after the party.*

2  .................... *obj* If you .................... something **out** to someone you direct their attention to it • *The saleswoman* .................... **out** *all the new features of the hi-fi.*

3  .................... *v* to move or travel towards the speaker or with the speaker • *Can Zoe* .................... **out** (.................... *with me*) *to play?* .................... *to leave a place* • *Nightfall is when vampires* .................... **out**, *thirsty for human blood.*

4  .................... *obj v* to test (something) to see if it is suitable or useful or if it works • .................... **on** (= put on) *the shoes to see if they fit.*

5  .................... *obj* to (cause to) become, change into or come to be (something) *It* .................... **out** (= it is now known, although it was not before) *that she had known him when they were children.*

6  .................... *obj* to move (something or someone) from one place to another • *If the dress is too small, you can* .................... *it* **back** *to the shop and get a refund.*

7  .................... *obj v* to take (something) out of or away from a place, esp. using physical effort. *I hadn't seen a dentist for three years and she had to* .................... *two of my teeth* **out**.

8  .................... *obj* to put (something) in order • *The kitchen's in a terrible mess and I don't want to go out until I've* .................... **up** (tidied it).

# Writing

## Discursive compositions

A student has been asked to write a composition for a school magazine with the following title: *The community suffers when small shops close.*

The student has completed some of the composition but needs help with the unfinished parts.

**1** Look at the notes that the student has made for the opening section. Write the opening section in three or four lines.

**2** The student has started the middle section by talking about the problems caused for local communities. Finish this section.

**3** The student has mentioned two solutions to the problem but does not say how this will help or who is going to make them work. Add your own ideas.

**4** The student has made a few notes for the concluding lines. Read the composition again and write the conclusion in two sentences.

---

*shopping centres opening everywhere / small shops closing but local community?*

The closing of small local shops can cause many problems for a community. Local shops can be a place for neighbours to meet and make people feel they live in a neighbourhood. They make life easier, for example, for parents with small children. The people who suffer the most when local shops disappear, however, are old people.

One way of preventing small shops from closing would be to give certain kinds of shops financial help to stay open. Every neighbourhood, for example, should have a post office, a chemist's and a newsagent's. Another solution would be to make it possible for such small shops to open next door to each other.

*big shops – range + low prices – small shops can't compete but are an important part of community*

---

# Grammar

## Transitive and intransitive verbs

**1** Look at this letter written to a problem page and the reply published in the magazine. There are brackets after the *italicised* verbs. Where the brackets contain words, decide whether any of them need to be crossed out; where they are empty decide whether any words need to be added to make the text grammatically correct.

## Service with a smile?

Dear Harvey,

A month ago, a couple of tiles *fell* (**1** .............................) the shower stall in the upstairs room. I couldn't *glue* (**2** to them) back in, because it's wet there and they wouldn't *stick* (**3** .............................).
So Mary tried to get a tile guy out to *fix* (**4** .............................). Tile guy number one said he wouldn't even *look* (**5** at the job) because it *sounded* (**6** .............................) too small. Tile guy number two said he'd be there before noon on Saturday, but he never *turned up* (**7** .............................). When Mary finally *reached* (**8** to him), he said he had decided to put up his storm windows, and that task took priority. Tile guy number three actually put in an appearance, poked around a little until another couple of tiles fell out, he *broke* (**9** .............................), *left* (**10** .............................) and said he'd *call* (**11** us with an estimate). No call. And he doesn't *return* (**12** us calls).

Homer Wilson

Dear Homer,

I can't help you, but yes, I *feel* (**13** you your pain). Ever wonder why service stations still have the word 'service' in their title? You run your own credit card through the slot at the pump, you *fill* (**14** the tank yourself) and wash your own windows. The only 'service' the station provides is to *sell* (**15** to you a lottery ticket). What bank *answers* (**16** to its phone) with a real live person? The message I hate most is 'Please *stay* (**17** on the line). Your call is important to us.' If the call is so important, you'd think they wouldn't want a machine to *take* (**18** .............................).

Harvey's moral: Bad service *saves* (**19** money to you) and *loses* (**20** customers). Good service *costs* (**21** money) and *saves* (**22** for you customers).

## 9

**2** **exam task** For questions 1–10, read the text below and think of the word which best fits each space. Use only one word in each space.

### Another shopping disaster

One Saturday I went **(1)** ............................ town with my mum. We were **(2)** ............................ around Benetton when I picked **(3)** ............................ something to show my mum. We got distracted **(4)** ............................ something else and a minute **(5)** ............................ left the shop. We walked **(6)** ............................ British Home Stores and I realised I was **(7)** ............................ carrying something – it was the shirt **(8)** ............................ Benetton. I quickly ran back, **(9)** ............................ it up and ran straight back **(10)** ............................ again. I was really embarrassed.

**3** Look at the following situations. Using *all* the words given and adding any others you think necessary, write a sentence that expresses the idea of the situation described. You may need to change the words given.

EXAMPLE: I've never taken my car anywhere else.
*I've always had my car repaired there.*
**have always repair there**

1 Three months ago your father asked a local shop to start delivering newspapers.
**have newspapers deliver three months**

2 The last time you went to the hairdresser's was six weeks ago.
**have hair cut six weeks**

3 You went to the garage but the car wash was closed.
**not have car clean**

4 You are advising a friend not to use a photographer's because it's expensive.
**not have develop there**

5 You are telling a friend her car isn't worth repairing.
**bother have repair**

6 Your tooth is hurting. It's got to come out.
**got have tooth take**

## Vocabulary

**Packaging and containers**

**1** What kind of packaging or containers do you usually find the following things in? Match a word on the left to at least two words on the right.

| | | |
|---|---|---|
| jar | | coffee |
| | | milk |
| tube | | sardines |
| | | margarine |
| carton | | coke |
| | | toothpaste |
| tin | **of** | ice cream |
| | | honey |
| packet | | shampoo |
| | | sun cream |
| can | | tonic water |
| | | tomatoes |
| sachet | | orange juice |
| | | flour |
| tub | | pasta |
| | | jam |

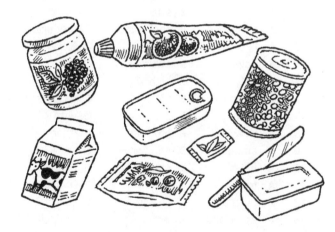

**2** Each of the gapped words below is a noun that can be used with both the items that follow. Add the missing letters as shown in the example:

a b $\underline{a}$ $\underline{l}$ $\underline{l}$ of string / wool

1 a _ _ _ r of chocolate / soap

2 a _ u _ _ _ _ of grapes / flowers

3 a _ _ _ _ _ e of luggage / furniture

4 a _ a _ _ _ of trousers / shorts

5 a _ _ _ _ c _ of bread / cheese

6 a c _ _ _ _ of ice / sugar

7 a _ _ _ _ _ k of celery / cinnamon

8 a p _ _ _ _ of glasses / gloves

**3** ⬛ **exam task** For questions 1–14, read the text below and decide which answer **A, B, C** or **D** best fits each space. There is an example at the beginning (0).

### Shopping in Thailand

Thailand is one of the best (0) B̲. for shopping in Asia. Not for duty-free (1) ..... such as cameras and electrical (2) ..... but for exquisite local handicrafts. (3) ..... in fixed price stores, it is normal to bargain. Try to obtain 15–20% (4) ..... . Credit cards are (5) ..... accepted. If shipping things you buy, keep your (6) ..... . In case of complaint, contact the Thai Authority for Tourists. Better still, buy in places recommended (7) ..... TAT, which should (8) ..... a sign.

Don Muang airport has a limited (9) ..... of duty-free shopping. Prices are usually (10) ..... than shops. Profiting (11) ..... the large number of tourists, shops at Phuket airport often (12) ..... up to 30% more than local shops, (13) ..... for pearls. Never buy anything of (14) ..... in a hurry.

| 0 | A countries | B places | C windows | D airports |
|---|---|---|---|---|
| 1 | A brands | B sales | C goods | D offers |
| 2 | A machinery | B appliances | C produce | D stores |
| 3 | A Except | B Apart | C Nevertheless | D In case |
| 4 | A down | B away | C off | D out |
| 5 | A fully | B highly | C greatly | D widely |
| 6 | A refunds | B bills | C receipts | D labels |
| 7 | A from | B by | C with | D to |
| 8 | A show | B promote | C offer | D display |
| 9 | A amount | B number | C scale | D level |
| 10 | A fuller | B bigger | C higher | D richer |
| 11 | A from | B with | C of | D about |
| 12 | A purchase | B charge | C cost | D spend |
| 13 | A especially | B only | C uniquely | D famously |
| 14 | A cost | B price | C value | D wealth |

**4** 'Pay' or 'pay for'
Would you typically use the following words with 'pay' or 'pay for'?

| | |
|---|---|
| the bill | the shopping |
| the rent | a deposit |
| a meal | me the money |
| a mistake | the full price |

## Preparation for speaking

**1** Service situations
What do you think you might be asked in the following shop and service situations?
Write down what the shop assistant would say.

1 You give a shop assistant a £10 note for something which costs 30 pence.
Haven't ....................................?

2 You have just tried on a pair of shoes in a shoe shop.
Do ....................................?

3 You want a refund for a pullover that is too small. You hand back the pullover.
Have ....................................?

4 You have just sat down in a hairdresser's chair. The hairdresser is ready to start.
How ....................................?

5 You've just given in some photographs to be developed.
When ....................................?

6 You are talking to a receptionist about when a dentist can see you.
When ....................................?

**2** Shopping baskets
Go to a local supermarket and write down the exact names of eight different things. Make sure you write down the type of product, brand, special features, weight, etc. like this:
*500 g. Dame Luxury Swiss Chocolate*

Write down the exact price of each of the eight items and then add up the total. Bring your list of items to class together with the total. You will be playing a game called shopping baskets. You will have to show your list of products to the whole class and in groups they will have to guess the total cost.

# Exam focus  Paper 4 Listening

## Part 2 Note taking or blank filling

Before each task begins in the Listening paper in the exam, you are given about 45 seconds to read through the questions in the question booklet. Using this time effectively is important.

In a note-taking or blank-filling task, as well as writing down the *correct information*, the answer you write must also be *grammatically correct*. So when reading through the task before the listening starts you should:

● try to predict what sort of information goes in each gap
● think about what part of speech the word or phrase could be

**1** Look at this listening task.

   **a** Which piece of information do you think is needed in each gap?

     **a** type of crime     **e** part of the store
     **b** period of the year   **f** people
     **c** security measure    **g** action
     **d** place in the store

   **b** Now match one of these of parts of speech to each gap.

     **h** plural noun      **k** *-ing* participle + object
     **i** uncountable noun   **l** adverb (place)
     **j** *-ing* participle    **m** prepositional phrase (time)

You will hear a store detective talking about her work.
For questions 1–8, complete the sentences.

Most security cameras are positioned [_____ **1** ].
Bar coding and the electronic tagging of goods means that fewer [_____ **2** ] are needed around the store.
Other [_____ **3** ] are the best source of information about criminals in the store.
[_____ **4** ] are the area of the store that poses the most security problems.
People have been caught [_____ **5** ] up to eight items of clothing inside the store.
The biggest problem in the food section is people [_____ **6** ] before the checkout.
There are far more cases of [_____ **7** ] to deal with at Christmas time.
At Christmas and [_____ **8** ] we have to employ temporary staff to help with security.

**2** Now read this extract from the tapescript and see if your answers were correct.

**Interviewer:** So tell us about some of the problems you have with shoplifters at Pricebusters.

**Karen Jones:** Well, we like to think that we have the very best security measures in place. Stopping crime in the modern age means using the very latest technology so we employ a whole range of computer and surveillance equipment. The two most common forms of security in today's shops are security cameras, which are usually overhead, and connected to monitoring screens in a back room somewhere and the bar code label on goods. If a bar code label has not been screened at a checkout, an alarm will go off as someone tries to leave the shop. Because of this electronic system we do not now need to employ as many staff to track suspicious customers around the store. Good old-fashioned methods work well too. Shoppers often go up and tell a member of staff if someone else in the store is doing something illegal and we'll always have someone watching changing rooms where cameras of course are not allowed to go. As you can imagine this area of the store gives us our biggest security headache. It has been known for customers to walk out of changing rooms wearing as many as eight items of clothing. Another thing that is hard to detect is people actually consuming items while on our premises. In the food section it is almost impossible to prevent someone eating something once they have decided to do it. Then, of course some periods of the year are much worse than others. The number of people we catch shoplifting increases dramatically at Christmas time and during the sales – even though we practically give stuff away. We still need to recruit extra temporary security staff.

# 10 Crime

## Reading

**1** Fake or counterfeit goods can be found in most countries. What kind are often available in your country? Why do people buy them? Should they, in your opinion?

**2** Read the article to see some of the consequences of buying fake or counterfeit goods.

# Faking the labels and making the money

Only a fool pays big money for the real thing when you can get stuff on the street for a fraction of the price. No one's going to know the difference and besides, it doesn't do anyone any harm, does it?

Sadly it's not quite that simple. Counterfeit goods are a serious problem for the big brand name manufacturers. 'Although none of the big companies would admit how much they are losing, it clearly runs into millions of pounds every year,' says John Anderson, executive secretary of the Anti-Counterfeiting Group, a body that represents around 200 major brands in the UK.

'You can buy a bag of fake Lacoste crocodiles in a market in some foreign country and just sew them on to a bunch of cheap T-shirts,' Anderson says. 'The products are often very poor quality, and you have no right to return those kinds of goods to the shop afterwards if they run in the wash or something.'

Although few people are likely to feel sorry for the brand name manufacturers, the problem goes deeper than that. 'A fake T-shirt is not going to kill you, but you could die if the profits from that shirt go into making fake pharmaceuticals. We have evidence that there is money-laundering going on and a lot of the profits often go back into drug-dealing,' says Anderson.

The Anti-Counterfeiting Group is convinced that most fake products are directly linked to organised crime and terrorism and there is strong anecdotal evidence to support this claim.

Trading of goods often works like this. The counterfeit traders operate from small portable crates, mostly selling fake perfumes and T-shirts. Three or four of them work a patch and the cash is held by a money man who watches over his team.

The money man hands out cash to his stooges, often women, who gather round the traders pretending to feverishly buy the fake goods. The stooge's job is to whip up interest from the public.

Each time the trader runs out of goods he gets more from a van parked out of sight nearby. At the first sign of trouble, the traders whip away their crates and disappear. Policing the counterfeiters is not easy.

So while the cunning counterfeiters continue to escape the law, black-market shoppers will still be able to look like a million dollars on the cheap. But at what cost to the rest of us?

**3** **exam task** For questions 1–6, choose the answer (A, B, C or D) which you think fits best according to the text.

1 The article claims that buying counterfeit goods

   A does little harm.
   B only harms big companies.
   C particularly harms women.
   D potentially harms everyone.

2 According to Mr Anderson big companies

   A deny they are losing money because of counterfeit goods.
   B are setting up an anti-counterfeit organisation.
   C buy their labels in foreign countries.
   D are losing a lot of money because of counterfeit goods.

3 The article suggests that

   A we should feel sorry for the big companies.
   B counterfeit goods help us look smart.
   C counterfeit goods are linked to other crimes.
   D counterfeit goods are made in foreign countries.

4 According to the article, counterfeit goods

   A are often sold from crates.
   B are good value for money.
   C are usually T-shirts.
   D are mainly bought by women.

5 The article claims

   A buying fake T-shirts can make us quite seriously ill.
   B drug-dealing may be financed by profits from fake goods.
   C some brand name manufacturers are linked to drug-dealing.
   D terrorists and drug-dealers depend on the public's ignorance.

6 According to the article, counterfeit trading is dependent on

   A good team work.
   B interest from the public.
   C quick reactions.
   D women's interest in shopping.

**4** Below are the steps in a counterfeit goods crime cycle. Read the article again to put them in the correct order.

profit made

fake T-shirts sold through teams of traders

profits used to finance organised crime and terrorism

profits used to make fake drugs

false labels put on cheap T-shirts

false labels bought

cheap T-shirts bought

**5** Make a list of the countable and uncountable nouns in the first two paragraphs of the article.

**6** In your opinion, are the dangers presented in this article realistic or exaggerated?

## Writing

### Planning discursive compositions

**1** Here is a discursive composition title: *Should people stop buying fake goods?*

Think about your opinion on this issue.

**2** Here is a plan for this composition, but it is in jumbled order. Work out the best order for the different parts.

a They are cheap / They let poorer people feel and look rich / Big brands make lots of money anyway

b A brief summary of my opinions

c A short statement about the current situation

d A sentence saying how the composition will be structured

e Fake goods steal their creator's ideas / Fake goods encourage organised crime

f My conclusion

**3** Make a list of some linking words and signposts that would be useful to join the main points above when writing this composition.

**4** Here is another discursive composition title. Write a plan for the composition.
*Young people who commit serious crimes should never be sent to prison.*

**5** **exam task** Write one of the compositions above in **120–180** words for your school magazine.

---

## Grammar

**1** Find six words related to crime from Unit 10 in the Student's Book or from a newspaper article. Then, with the help of a dictionary, write a definition of each word using this structure:
*This is someone who / something which ...*

EXAMPLE: *a pickpocket:*
*This is someone who steals things from people's pockets and bags.*

Bring your definitions to class, then get into teams and check the definitions. Each team should then take it in turns to read out their definitions. The other teams must guess the word that is being defined. The first team to guess gets a point. The team with the most points at the end is the winner.

**2** There are seven differences between the two pictures below. What are they? Find them and describe them to yourself. Remember about countable and uncountable nouns.

**3** **exam task** Read the text below and look carefully at each line. Some of the lines are correct, and some have a word which should not be there. If a line is correct put a tick (✓) by the line. If a line has a word which should not be there, write the word at the end of the line. There is an example at the beginning (0).

### Dyeing dogs blue proves expensive

| | | |
|---|---|---|
| **0** | Three young people appeared in the court today charged with dyeing three | *the* |
| **1** | dogs blue. The lawyer who she spoke for the prosecution explained that the | |
| **2** | crime had happened before a football match and that the colours of the | |
| **3** | home team were the same blue as the colour used to dye the dogs. She also | |
| **4** | called on two witnesses who they claimed to have seen the young people | |
| **5** | actually spraying the dogs with cans of paint. | |
| **6** | The defending lawyer, however, that argued the dogs actually belonged to | |
| **7** | the young people and called on some of neighbours who were able to give | |
| **8** | an evidence that this was the case. | |
| **9** | The judge in his summing up accepted that the dogs belonged to the young | |
| **10** | people but nevertheless found them guilty of a cruelty to animals. They | |
| **11** | were each ordered to pay a fine of £100 and to clean the dogs. | |

Which of the mistakes in this article are caused by using 'a' or 'an' with uncountable nouns?

## Vocabulary

**1** **exam task** Read the text below and decide which answer **A, B, C** or **D** best fits each space. There is an example at the beginning **(0)**.

### The mystery of the Mona Lisa

The paintings of Leonardo da Vinci have always attracted controversy. Only 14 works have ever been attributed to him and experts have **(0)** B. the authenticity of several. Not even the Mona Lisa is above **(1)** ...... . The painting is neither signed nor dated and no **(2)** ..... of payment to Leonardo has ever been found. Believed to be the portrait of the wife of Florentine merchant Francesco del Gioconda dating from 1502, it has been on public **(3)** ..... in the Louvre since 1804. Now housed in a bullet- **(4)** ..... glass case, it has always been surrounded by **(5)** ..... security.

Even so, on 24th August 1911, it was **(6)** ..... . Initial leads came to nothing and no **(7)** ..... to the thief's motives or the whereabouts of the picture materialised for 15 months. In November 1913, Florentine art dealer Alfredo Geri received a letter from someone **(8)** ..... they had the Mona Lisa and were prepared to sell it back to Italy for 500,000 lire. Geri contacted the director of the Uffizi museum who arranged a meeting with the alleged vendor.

He turned out to be an Italian carpenter Vincenzo Peruggia, who made the painting's **(9)** ..... wooden box for the Louvre and was able to steal it because he knew the museum's **(10)** ...... .The Mona Lisa he produced was proclaimed genuine by the Uffizi and sent back to Paris. But a British conman, Jack Dean, later insisted that he had helped Peruggia steal the painting but **(11)** ..... a copy before Peruggia took it to Italy. Could it be that the painting seen by thousands of visitors every day in the Louvre museum is a total **(12)** ..... ?

| 0 | **A** asked | **B** questioned | **C** wondered | **D** enquired |
|---|---|---|---|---|
| 1 | **A** question | **B** doubt | **C** query | **D** suspicion |
| 2 | **A** record | **B** document | **C** receipt | **D** bill |
| 3 | **A** exhibition | **B** show | **C** display | **D** sight |
| 4 | **A** secure | **B** strong | **C** guard | **D** proof |
| 5 | **A** careful | **B** accurate | **C** safe | **D** tight |
| 6 | **A** stolen | **B** thieved | **C** burgled | **D** pickpocketed |
| 7 | **A** indications | **B** clues | **C** hints | **D** tips |
| 8 | **A** claiming | **B** pretending | **C** arguing | **D** persuading |
| 9 | **A** surrounding | **B** protective | **C** closed | **D** fake |
| 10 | **A** security | **B** working | **C** doors | **D** routine |
| 11 | **A** substituted | **B** replaced | **C** copied | **D** taken over |
| 12 | **A** false | **B** substitute | **C** counterfeit | **D** fake |

## Preparation for speaking

**1** Can you distinguish between these two sounds: /æ/ (as in 'had') and /ɑː/ (as in 'hard')?

Look at this set of words in which the two sounds are contrasted, and practise saying them out loud.

| | | |
|---|---|---|
| had / hard | hat / heart | bat / Bart |
| pat / part | ban / barn | pack / park |
| cat / cart | ham / harm | |

**2** Here are two watches. Are they the same? Could either of them be a fake? Look at them and make notes about the differences and any evidence of forgery. Be prepared to speak about the watches and give your opinions in class.

# *Exam focus*  Paper 5 Speaking

## Part 2 Individual long turn

The exam task below needs to be carried out in groups of three. You may wish to prepare for it individually at home before you carry it out in class.

**exam task** Talk about these photos in groups of three: two candidates and an interlocutor. The interlocutor should lead the conversation using the instructions below.

### For Candidate A

Now, I'd like each of you to talk on your own for about a minute.

I'm going to give each of you two different photographs and I'd like you to talk about them.

Candidate A, here are your two photographs. They show two different film posters. Please let Candidate B see them. Candidate B, I'll give you your photos in a minute.

Candidate A, I'd like you to compare and contrast these photos, saying which film you'd rather see and why. Remember, you have only about a minute for this so don't worry if I interrupt you. All right?

*(After approximately one minute)* Thank you. Candidate B, which film would you rather see?

### For Candidate B

Candidate B, here are your two photographs. They show young people in different places. Please let Candidate A see them.

Candidate B, I'd like you to compare and contrast these photos, saying which you think is a better way for the teenagers to spend their time. Remember, you have only about a minute for this so don't worry if I interrupt you. All right?

*(After approximately one minute)* Thank you. Candidate A, which place would you rather be in?

# 11 Transport

## Reading

**1** How do you think planes and flying might change in the next ten years? Note down your thoughts, then see if the article below mentions these too.

**2** What changes in planes and flying does the article predict? Do you think they are a good idea or really likely to happen?

### Get the plane out of the garage, will you – I'm late for work

Forget a Jaguar or a Porsche. If you really want to impress your friends the vehicle you should be saving for is not a car to get stuck in traffic jams, but your very own 'personal plane'.

In just three years' time, these cheaper (around £25,000), simpler aircraft could encourage thousands of people to pilot themselves to work, along what experts describe as 'highways in the sky'. 'Personal planes could revolutionise air travel,' says Keith Henry of NASA's research centre in Virginia, USA. **0** **H**

Personal planes are just one of a series of next-generation planes now under development, guaranteed to make flying faster and cheaper than ever. **1** Already, engineers are designing craft which could fly from London to New York in an hour. Alternatively you could take your own plane out of the garage and commute to work.

Personal plane technology has been in development since 1994, when NASA, the US Federal Aviation Authority and a consortium of 75 American companies started to work on a project to develop cheap user-friendly aircraft. **2**

Don't worry: you won't need a degree in rocket science to fly one of these planes. Bruce Holmes, general aviation manager for NASA says the aircraft will be almost as simple to fly as a car is to drive. **3** The huge number of dials and devices used to fly existing planes won't be needed.

**4** To fly to Rome, for example, you will just touch the relevant departure and destination airports on a computer and the best route will be chosen and a flight plan automatically filed with air traffic controllers.

Experts are convinced personal planes will be as safe as other modes of transport as various special features will facilitate this. **5** In case you'd rather rely on someone else but find today's planes a bit uncomfortable and boring, rest assured: the interiors of jets are set to change. **6** All airlines are racing to improve their flight entertainment: several already give many passengers their own small video screen, a choice of movies and games, and soon you will be able to surf the web as you fly.

**3** **exam task** Seven sentences have been removed from the article. Choose from the sentences A–H the one which fits each gap (1–6). There is one extra sentence which you do not need to use. There is an example at the beginning (0).

**A** British military scientists are helping develop deadly planes so fast only robots can fly them.

**B** These will include huge airbags, computerisation of all the most complicated procedures and use of special materials to make the aircraft lighter and stronger.

**C** This will eventually enable ordinary people to actually think of owning their own planes and flying them around.

**D** Two firms are already launching planes with new cockpit technology developed through the project.

**E** Virgin Atlantic is considering plans to operate casinos on board long haul planes, complete with double beds for the wealthiest passengers.

**F** To increase speed when airborne, for example, the pilot will push on the throttle just as a driver would press an accelerator in a car.

**G** Navigation will be as easy as pressing a button.

**H** This is the base for much of the research into the new planes.

**4** Underline all the examples in the article of the future tense with 'will' (both positive and negative). Why is 'will' used so much in the article rather than 'may' or 'going to'?

**5** Underline six vocabulary items in the article related to flying.

**6** Would you like to have a personal plane? What would you like it to be able to do?

## Writing

**Formality of language in report writing**

**1** Here is part of a report of a school trip to London. It is written for a class teacher by a student who went on the trip. In some places two alternative ways of saying the same thing are given, one quite formal and the other less formal. Read through the report and underline the less formal alternatives. These are more likely in this context.

**2** Now rewrite this as a report from the school head to the bus company. It should be quite formal. To help you, use the information about formal and informal features of writing on pages 144–5 of Unit 11 in the Student's Book.

---

### Report on school trip of March 31st to London

**TRANSPORT**

We hired a bus for the trip. The service provided by the bus company was really bad. Because of it, the amount of time **(1) available / we had** for looking round London was **(2) reduced / cut** by two hours, and we got home late and hungry, **(3) causing concern to our parents / making our parents worried. (4) Details are as follows / Here are the details:**

1 The bus **(5) arrived at / got to** the school **(6) about / approximately** one hour late in the morning.

2 The bus company's enquiry hotline didn't answer when we rang to find out what had happened.

3 The bus obviously hadn't been cleaned since it was last used – it was **(7) really / extremely** dirty and smelly.

4 The bus driver was extremely **(8) discourteous / rude** and unhelpful – he **(9) offered no apologies / didn't say sorry** for being late and refused to take alternative routes when the bus **(10) was caught up / got stuck** in traffic jams.

We really shouldn't pay the company for this service. They should also **(11) give back / refund** our deposit and give us some compensation for all the **(12) hassle / inconvenience.**

---

## Grammar

**1** Think about what you know about when flying first started, e.g. who was the first person to fly? What kind of plane was it? When was it? Then read the article to see if you were right. Note the date of the article.

**2** **exam task** Read the article again and think of the word which best fits each space. Use only one word in each space. There is an example at the beginning (0).

**3** Imagine you watched this first flight. Practise speaking by briefly giving a description of what you saw to an imaginary friend.

### Brothers take to the air
#### North Carolina, 17 December 1903

It lasted for only 12 seconds, and the fragile machine in which he rode rose only ten feet above the ground and covered **(0)** *barely*. 120 feet (37 metres) from start to finish, but today on the sand dunes near Kitty Hawk, North Carolina, man **(1)** ............... taken wings and made his first-ever powered flight.

The brothers Orville and Wilbur Wright, bicycle mechanics from Dayton, Ohio have **(2)** ............... moving steadily towards today's flights since 1890 when they began looking at hitherto unsuccessful **(3)** ............... to fly. After experimenting with gliders they realised that the secret lay in rigid, airworthy wings. **(4)** ............... exhaustive testing of every part of their proposed flying machine, the Wrights came to Kitty Hawk. **(5)** ............... Orville lying face down in a cradle beneath **(6)** ............... wings, and the elder brother, Wilbur, running alongside, *Flyer 1*, powered **(7)** ............... its 12 mph engine, moved along its supports, then, as the wind caught **(8)** ............... , the flying machine gently rose upwards into the wind. The Wrights made three further flights before their machine **(9)** ............... damaged by a sudden gust of wind. The longest **(10)** ............... for 59 seconds and covered 852 feet.

**4** Complete these sentences with the most appropriate past modal *(may / must / might / can't / should / could + have)* and the correct form of the verb in brackets according to your opinion.

1  The Wright brothers .................................... (be) very courageous.
   The Wright brothers ...*must have been*... very courageous.

2  Orville Wright .................................... (feel) both fear and excitement together as he lay in the cradle in the first flight.

3  The cradle .................................... (keep) its passenger warm and comfortable.

4  The Wright brothers .................................... (inspire) by Leonardo da Vinci.

5  The Wrights .................................... (make) their first flight from a mountain top to get more height and wind.

6  If the Wright brothers had had more money they .................................... (fly) earlier.

7  The Wrights .................................... (consider) many kinds of design before making their final decision.

**5** Imagine you lived in 1903 and witnessed this first flight. Write a letter to a friend describing what you saw, and talking about its importance and what you predict it might mean for the future.

# Vocabulary

## Getting around places

**1** Here is a transport map of London showing how you can get around the centre. Find some famous places on the map and see how you could travel from one place to another.

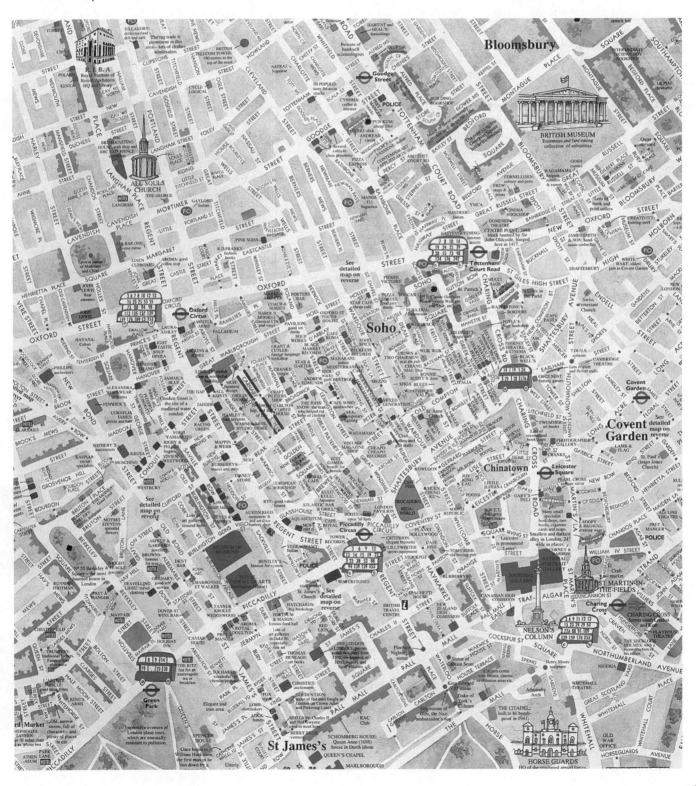

**2** Read this extract from a guidebook about travelling round London. Choose the correct word from the list below for each gap (1–9).

> valid   jam   reliability   double-deckers   fares
> conductor   platform   ticket   request

The fastest way of getting around the city is by **Underground**, or **Tube**, as it is known to all Londoners. Operating from about 5.30am until shortly after midnight, the eleven lines cross much of the city, although south of the river is not well covered and the **(1)** ................................... of certain lines (such as the notorious Northern) is often lousy. Tickets are bought from machines or from a **(2)** ................................... booth in the station entrance hall. Savings can be made on **(3)** ................................... by purchasing a **Travelcard**, on sale from machines and ticket booths at all tube stations as well as from some newsagents. Travelcards are **(4)** ................................... for as many journeys as you want and can also be used on buses and suburban rail networks.

The network of **buses** is very dense, but you will soon find that the tube is generally quicker, especially in the summer when central London becomes one large traffic **(5)** ................................... . Normally you pay the driver on entering, although some routes – especially those through the centre – are covered by older buses with an open rear **(6)** ................................... and staffed by a **(7)** ................................... . A lot of bus stops are **(8)** ................................... stops, so if you don't stick your arm out, the bus will drive on. While the majority of London's buses are still the distinctive red **(9)** ................................... , an increasing number of routes are now served by different coloured and sized buses.

**3** Now complete the next paragraph from the same guidebook with the correct prepositions.

If you're **(1)** ................................... a group of three or more, London's metered **black cabs** can be an economical way **(2)** ................................... getting around the centre of town. A yellow light **(3)** ................................... the windscreen tells you if the cab is available – just stick your arm **(4)** ................................... to hail it. London's cabbies are the best trained in Europe – every one of them knows the shortest route **(5)** ................................... any two points **(6)** ................................... the capital, and won't rip you **(7)** ................................... by taking another route.

## Preparation for speaking

Here are two different photos. Prepare to compare and contrast them and say how you feel about getting around by these two means of transport. Organise your thoughts, and think about what language you will need to use.

Look at the Speaking sections of the Student's Book to find useful language for comparing and contrasting.

# Exam focus Paper 1 Reading

## Part 3 Gapped text

**exam task** You are going to read an extract from a short story about a couple arriving in London as immigrants. Six paragraphs have been removed from the extract. Choose from the paragraphs A–G the one which fits each gap 1–5. There is one extra paragraph which you do not need to use. There is an example at the beginning (0).

The immigration lady explained to us how to get to the bed and breakfast. 'I will put you on the train from here and you will have to go up to London Victoria Station. When you arrive at London Victoria, you may change either to the Victoria Line, then to the Piccadilly Line, and get off at Hammersmith. Or you may take the District Line from Victoria up to Hammersmith if you prefer.

**0** | G

'Alternatively,' she said, 'you may take the Victoria Line and change to the Central Line, then go up to Shepherd's Bush station. When you arrive there, get out and take the number 207 bus. The number 207 bus will also take you up near to the bed and breakfast hostel where you are supposed to go and stay.'

**1** |

The immigration lady finished her briefing about the location of the bed and breakfast hostel and took us down to the trains. At the platform there was already a train waiting to leave in a few minutes' time.

**2** |

We sat in the train for a few minutes waiting for it to leave. I closed my eyes and started to contrast the trains back at home in Uganda to the British train we were currently sitting in.

**3** |

I must have looked downcast. But she reassured us that it was OK. She said, 'It's faster by train than by bus. It is the easiest and quickest means of transportation here in the UK.'

'Is it?' I asked.

'Oh yes, it is.'

**4** |

The first impression was marvellous. The seats were smart. There was no overcrowding. There were no domestic animals or agricultural produce being ferried inside it alongside the passengers. The condition of the Gatwick Express train did not turn out to be as we had feared.

**5** |

**C** I exclaimed at the idea of travelling by train because back at home in Uganda people hardly travel that way. I started to think of the risks, the inconveniences and the difficulties that people who use the train there always face. Travelling by train in Uganda means travelling in the company of an assortment of livestock including cattle, goats, pigs and chickens – just to mention a few – and not forgetting a range of agricultural produce. So I thought that travelling by train here would also be full of such hazards. Fortunately it didn't seem to be the same case here in the British train.

**D** We quickly realised that we were in a new world, Great Britain. We were in a developed world, much more developed than our country, Uganda, which had been ravaged by brutal civil wars. It was inevitable for us to make such comparisons and contrasts. Without them it would be difficult for us to understand the full meaning of development when people spoke of it.

**E** When I'd heard the immigration lady talk to us about taking the train, I'd said to myself, 'By train?' I thought I'd said it to myself. But it seemed I'd said it aloud and the immigration lady heard me. She answered, 'Yes, by train. You will have to travel by train.'

**F** Although we had realised that coming to another country would mean seeing many kinds of differences, we hadn't really understood exactly how different things could actually be. The immigration lady similarly seemed to have little idea of how far apart two countries could be.

**G** 'Whichever line you choose to travel on, take it up to Hammersmith station and then get off. When you come out of the station take the number 266 bus. It will take you near to where the bed and breakfast hostel is.'

**A** The explanation given by the immigration lady was difficult to master. However, we listened to it all very carefully. Imagine all those details given to be mastered by newly arrived asylum-seekers who haven't been in the country before, who have not come under any normal circumstances and therefore are far from relaxed, people who may be thinking that they're being followed or are filled with uncertainty about their future. We decided that the immigration lady must have taken it for granted that, because we were highly educated, we would experience no difficulties in finding our way through the meandering maze of the city to the bed and breakfast hostel in west London. But it seemed to us like a very big challenge to undertake.

**B** The immigration lady saw us on to the train and then she wished us good luck. She waved goodbye to us for a few seconds, smiling, and then she went back to her office. When she left I asked Frederick, 'Do you think we will make it?' Frederick answered, 'I don't know. Anyway, we will try.'

# 12 The media

## Reading

**1** You are going to read a text about the TV programme Baywatch. First read these sentences and decide whether the highlighted words refer to a word or idea in the sentence itself or something in a different part of the text in **2**.

**A** The cast stop filming once they get ankle deep in water.

**B** They are always tearfully reunited with their grateful parents.

**C** There's a vital flaw: the rescue teams seem rather overdressed.

**D** They're certainly not throwing it away on the costume budget, are they?

**E** It was Baywatch's British fans who saved it.

**F** Meanwhile, lifeguards Shauni (Erica Eleniak) and Eddie (Billy Warlock) saved sun-worshipping women from over-exposure as they uncovered a plot to sell organic fibre swimsuits that disintegrate in the water.

**G** This always gives them the shock of their lives.

**H** This always ends with him rugby-tackling the main villain.

**I** Each episode, in fact, is enjoyed by more than one billion people.

**2** As you read the text below, work out what the highlighted words in the sentences in **1** might refer to.

**exam task** You are going to read an article about a TV programme. Eight sentences have been removed from the article. Choose from the sentences A–H the one which fits each gap (1–7). There is one extra sentence which you do not need to use. There is an example at the beginning (0).

## Baywatch

Whichever way you turn, you can't get away from Baywatch: Hollywood's answer to a costume drama is now the world's most watched programme. **0** I

It wasn't always popular, though: in 1989 NBC cut the show. **1** It was rescued by LWT and the personal investment of its star, David Hasselhoff. He was already known in the UK from the adventure series Knight Rider, in which he co-starred with a talking car.

**The cost:** Baywatch costs $800,000 per episode, cut from $1.2 million, which still seems excessive when you consider it's mainly filmed on a beach with actors in swimwear. **2**

**The plot:** A typical episode has three plot strands. In one, a guest star might be struggling to make it as a singer while working as a waitress and on the run from her psychopathic former boyfriend. In the second strand, a lifeguard recovering from alcoholism might be visited by a dark figure from his past. The third strand will involve head lifeguard Hasselhoff foiling a plot to pollute the beach, for example. **3**

Teenagers from the wrong part of town are a regular feature. They learn from the lifeguards that there is more to life than hanging around with a bad crowd. **4**

**Yesterday's episode:** Mitch (Hasselhoff) was reunited with his nomadic brother, Buzzy, and wayward nephew, Kyle, during the annual surfing contest. Not only did Mitch restore peace between father and son, but he also rescued Kyle from a near-fatal attempt to surf near a condemned pier. **5**

**Rescues per episode:** Four. This means that the six lifeguards who patrol the half mile of Baywatch beach carry out 208 rescues per year.

**The reality:** **6** They move to a beach further down the coast. Santa Monica Bay is so polluted with toxic and human waste that the cast were falling victim to vomiting, skin, ear and eye infections.

**Newspaper latest:** An American TV company is hoping to repeat the success of Baywatch with a series about a mountain rescue service in the Rockies. **7**

**3** Look at these statements about the Baywatch programme.
In each one there is a highlighted word or phrase. Replace this
word or phrase with a similar one that was used in the text.

1 Each show is filmed at two different locations.
2 The hero Mitch has been involved in several
  accidents in which he could have died.
3 Guest stars often appear on the programme.
4 There's no escaping Baywatch: it is everywhere.
5 The actors in Baywatch don't actually swim in Santa
  Monica Bay.
6 A typical plot is one where Mitch and his friends help
  sort out problems between family members.

## Writing

In the Reading section above, we saw how 'reference' words help readers to
make connections between ideas in sentences. Such words are important
features of articles and reports.

**1** The following words are useful when referring to two people or things.
Complete the gaps in this article about twins with these words.

> the other    both    each
> neither    their    they
> each other

**2** There are three points in the
article marked with **. This
marks a point where the
writer has avoided repeating
unnecessary words because the
reader can fill these in from the
context. What words was it
unnecessary to repeat?

Twin sisters **Terry Connolly** and **Margaret Richardson** were
born on St Valentine's Day, 1943, in Leicester. Margaret was
adopted at six weeks old, Terry ** at eight months so that
**(1)** ................... was aware of **(2)** ...................'s existence until 1978.
Yet a number of coincidences linked **(3)** ................... separate lives.
**(4)** ................... had married on the same Saturday of the same year
(1960) within an hour of **(5)** ................... . **(6)** ................... planned to
have four children who were conceived and ** born at
approximately the same time. The eldest child of **(7)** ...................
was 11, the youngest ** 3. **(8)** ................... both liked the name
Ruth. Margaret's first daughter was called Ruth. Terry had wanted
to name her daughter Ruth but was dissuaded because unpleasant
neighbours had a daughter of the same name.

**3** This article is about a different set of twins. Each time they are referred to, their names are used. The article also repeats information that is unnecessary. Improve the article to make it easier to read. Replace the names with the reference words from **1**, where appropriate, and rewrite sections to avoid unnecessary repetition.

Identical twins **Bridget Harrison** of Leicester and **Dorothy Lowe** of Blackburn were separated only weeks after Bridget's and Dorothy's birth in 1945. Bridget and Dorothy did not meet until 1979. Neither Bridget nor Dorothy had known she was a twin but Bridget and Dorothy's lives had formed remarkable parallels. Bridget had married within a year of Dorothy, Dorothy had married within a year of Bridget. Bridget had named Bridget's son Andrew Richard, while Dorothy had named Dorothy's son Richard Andrew. Dorothy's daughter was called Catherine Louise and Bridget's daughter Karen Louise (Bridget had wanted to call Bridget's daughter Catherine but had changed Bridget's daughter's name to Karen to please a relative). Both Bridget and Dorothy had cats called Tiger and Dorothy and Bridget had studied the piano to the same grade. When reunited, Dorothy and Bridget had seven rings on Dorothy's and Bridget's hands and Dorothy and Bridget wore the same perfume. But perhaps the biggest coincidence of all was that Bridget and Dorothy had kept diaries for one year only – 1960. Bridget's diary and Dorothy's diary were of the same make, type and colour, and Bridget and Dorothy had each faithfully made entries for exactly the same number of days before stopping.

# Grammar

**Future forms**

**1** Choose the correct ending for each sentence from the alternatives given on the right. In each case, only one is correct. Think carefully about the future idea in each sentence.

| | | |
|---|---|---|
| 1 | By the time you get e-mail | it is being old-fashioned. / they will have invented something else. |
| 2 | It looks as though | he's going to win. / he'll be winning. |
| 3 | For the next few weeks | she'll be working as a DJ. / she'll have appeared on TV. |
| 4 | Shall I check what's on | or do you? / or are you going? / or will you? |
| 5 | I really don't think | I'll have time to go out this week. / I'm having the time this week. |
| 6 | I'm determined that | you are not preventing me. / you are not going to prevent me. |
| 7 | Why not come round if | you're not doing anything later / you will not do anything later? |
| 8 | Can you post this if | you will go to the post office? / you are going to the post office? |
| 9 | I'll call you as soon as | I will get there. / I get there. |
| 10 | I was wondering whether you | will go out tomorrow. / are doing anything tomorrow. |

## 2 Tense review

Here is an extract from a magazine feature about 'clever excuses'. Put the verb in brackets into the correct tense.

**'My dog ate it'** – no such lame excuses for smart people. Our selection of real-life excuses is packed with drama and deception.

I (1) ..................... (take) risks with a particular college course all year and couldn't afford to make one more mistake. I overslept and (2) ..................... (miss) the final exam. I knew I (3) ..................... (need) an amazing excuse, so I called my professor and told her that I (4) ..................... (leave) my contact lenses in too long, (5) ..................... (burn) my eyes and was temporarily blinded. I then (6) ..................... (ask) my sister, who's a nurse, to write a note verifying my condition. The professor believed me but decided that my studying should not go to waste. So she (7) ..................... (ask) me to come in for an oral exam. I wore patches on my eyes and (8) ..................... (have) to have someone lead me into the office as if I were blind.
*Louise, 22*

I (9) ..................... (speed) when a policeman (10) ..................... (come) out of nowhere and pulled me over. Any more points and I (11) ..................... (lose) my licence. So I told the officer that I was a surgeon and I was late for an operation that I (12) ..................... (perform). Unfortunately, he (13) ..................... (insist) on escorting me to the hospital which was 10 miles away in the opposite direction.
*Andrew, 33*

This new man I (14) ..................... (go) out with really wanted to meet my parents but I knew my mother (15) ..................... (hate) him. So I told him they both (16) ..................... (work) for the International Red Cross and were in Zaire indefinitely. But then he became interested in Zaire and started asking me all about it. I can't believe I (17) ..................... (know) so much about a country I (18) ..................... (never/visit).
*Anna, 23*

## Vocabulary

**1** **exam task** For questions 1–12, read the text below and decide which answer **A, B, C** or **D** best fits each space. There is an example at the beginning (0).

### CNN breeds nation of news junkies

If the end of the world ever comes, it seems (0) C. to assume that most of America will be glued to its television (1) ..... and tuned to CNN as the final hour approaches. Largely thanks to CNN and its imitators, the United States is more than ever a nation of news junkies. Over the past decade and a half, the vast (2) ..... for the traditional news (3) ..... of CBS, ABC and NBC has slowly dwindled as (4) ..... and listeners tune (5) ..... to 'Get it first, get it fast, get it now!' as one all-news radio (6) ..... puts it. In times of crisis or high (7) ..... like the exploding space shuttle Challenger or the Gulf War, America automatically turns to CNN. In bars, airports, aircraft, hotel lobbies, corner shops and anywhere else where people might pause and (8) ..... , the news pours out in a steady stream.

The news is no longer a series of (9) ..... to be explained and analysed nightly by a set of experts, but increasingly a form of vivid, instant (10) ..... . 'The news is always changing,' CNN's jingle says, 'so tune in two, three, four times a day.' If you do not, it is implied, you may (11) ..... something, an important (12) ..... in the endless soap opera that is real life.

| | A | B | C | D |
|---|---|---|---|---|
| 0 | well | sure | safe | strong |
| 1 | controls | sets | monitors | boxes |
| 2 | crowd | audience | people | public |
| 3 | broadcasts | shows | series | performances |
| 4 | spectators | observers | viewers | witnesses |
| 5 | on | over | up | in |
| 6 | channel | station | wave | speaker |
| 7 | theatre | action | drama | plot |
| 8 | watch | see | hear | notice |
| 9 | actions | events | occasions | signals |
| 10 | pastime | entertainment | enjoyment | leisure |
| 11 | lose | waste | miss | leave |
| 12 | series | piece | track | episode |

**2** **exam task** For questions 1–12, read the text below. Use the word in capitals given at the end of each line to form a word that fits in the space in the same line. There is an example at the beginning (0).

**INTERACTIVE TV**

Britain's armchair television (0) ..*critics*.. no longer have to suffer   **CRITICISM**
TV (1) .................. they don't like thanks to the world's first interactive   **COMEDY**
comedy show, Cosmic Comedy Interactive.

Devised by Videotron, the show follows the (2) .................. mix of   **TRADITION**
stand-up and satiric wit, with an extraordinary (3) .................. bonus.   **ADD**
Instead of sitting through the worst performers, the (4) .................. at   **VIEW**
home can (5) .................. to 'zap' with their remote control any of the   **CHOICE**
would-be stars and bring on a new one. Videotron's set-top box (6) ..................   **ABLE**
you to switch between any one of four channels creating the (7) ..................   **IMPRESS**
of (8) .................. .   **INTERACTIVE**

Videotron says that interactive versions of Eurosport's Winter Olympics
(9) .................. and interactive programmes in general attract far bigger   **COVER**
audiences than 'linear' shows. It claims that the number of (10) ..................   **CANCEL**
of cable (11) .................. after trying the new interactive product is   **SUBSCRIBE**
(12) .................. reduced.   **DRAMA**

# Preparation for speaking

**1** Here are some famous slips made by TV and radio commentators. In class you will be asked to discuss with another student what makes them funny.

**1** **Sports commentator:** *'That's a wise substitution by the manager: three fresh men, three fresh legs.'*

**2** **Athlete:** *'I've got ten pairs of trainers. That's one for every day of the week.'*

**3** **Presenter:** *So you haven't won the TV then, but what would you have done with it?*
**Contestant:** *Er ... watched it.*

**4** **Radio psychologist:** *So you were an only child. Do you know why?*
**Caller:** *Because my parents didn't have any more children.*

**5** **Sports commentator:** *'... and that bronze medal is worth its weight in gold.'*

**6** **Radio DJ:** *Disappointing news for Beethoven as his 9th Symphony drops nine places in our Hall of Fame.*

**7** **Presenter:** *'There are thousands of people out there who haven't claimed benefit for deafness because they haven't heard about it.'*

**8** **Caller:** *There are too many foreign players in the league.*
**Presenter:** *Why do you think that is?*
**Caller:** *Because there are a lot of them.*

**2** Look at this photograph of people arriving at a media event. Make notes to bring to class on these points.
- What do you think the event could be and what is going to take place?
- How would you feel at such an event?

*Exam focus* **Paper 2 Writing**

## Part 2 Articles

**1** Look at this exam question and the article that was written in response to it. Note that there are language mistakes in the article.

> A local paper is looking for articles on 'useful' TV programmes. Write an article which gives details of an informative TV programme you have recently seen. Your article should be between **120–180** words.

### Get Up and Go

I write to let you know about 'Get Up and Go' – the new holiday programme. I watch it every week and it's very entertaining. Never mind you don't want to go on holiday, it's just fun to see.

Each programme shows two different holidays. The presenters find the cheapest way to go somewhere and find what is there to do. They don't book hotels, etc. They arrive in a place and explore.

That's why called 'Get Up and Go'. However, it's useful too if you will go holidays and want to do something different. Like last week one presenter went cycling around Estonia. The week ago the other presenter went to help on a farm in Scotland. They show different things to do and problems you might have.

In conclusion, in each programme they show viewers' letters about places must avoid, give useful addresses of organisations and recommend cheap ways to do things. If you like journeys, you'll love this programme, so make an appointment to watch.

Evaluate the article, noting down at least one good point and one bad point for each category.

| | Good points | Bad points |
|---|---|---|
| CONTENT (*answering the question*) | | |
| RANGE OF LANGUAGE (*vocabulary and grammar*) | | |
| ORGANISATION (*order / linking*) | | |
| FORMAT (*like an article?*) | | |
| TARGET READER (*Would you want to watch the programme?*) | | |

**2** Now go through the article again and correct all the language mistakes.

**3** **exam task** A magazine for young people is looking for articles about 'the best or worst evening to stay in and watch TV'. Write an article giving your views on one evening's programmes. Your article should be between **120–180** words.

# 13 Lifestyles

## Reading

**1** You are going to read a text written by an American returning to the USA for the first time after living in Britain for several years. The text contains several words which are common in American English but not in British English. Look at the words listed below and match up pairs of words which mean the same thing in British English and American English.

> pavement   gas station   highway   parking lot
> sidewalk   car park   elevator   truck   motorway
> junction   lorry   garage   lift   intersection

**2** The things below are mentioned in the text in connection with American life:

> eating out   parking   getting around
> the average American   small towns

Write down one or two words that might describe each of these aspects of American life before you read the text. Think about what you have read in books or seen in films about America.

**3** Now read the text. Can you find any of the things you wrote in your list?

**4** As you do this exam task, find reasons in the text for rejecting the three wrong answers as well as choosing the one that you think is right.

**exam task** For questions 1–7, choose the answer (**A, B, C** or **D**) which you think fits best according to the text.

**1** The writer

   **A** has been to Carbondale once before.

   **B** thinks Carbondale has changed.

   **C** knows his way around Carbondale.

   **D** thinks Carbondale has no town centre.

**2** The writer thinks the people of Carbondale

   **A** look strange.

   **B** don't walk anywhere.

   **C** must be fitter than he is.

   **D** go to one shop for everything.

## THE AMERICAN WAY

I got a room in the Heritage Motor Inn, then went out once more to find Carbondale. But there was nothing there. There was no town, just six-lane highways and shopping malls. There weren't even any sidewalks. Going for a walk, as I discovered, was a ridiculous undertaking. I had to cross parking lots and garage forecourts, and I kept coming up against little white-painted walls marking the boundaries between, say, Long John Silver's Seafood Shoppe and Kentucky Fried Chicken. To get from one to the other, it was necessary to clamber over the wall, scramble up a grassy embankment and pick your way through a thicket of parked cars. That is if you were on foot. But clearly from the looks people gave me as I lumbered breathlessly over the embankment no one had ever tried to go from one of these places to another under his own motive power. What you were supposed to do was get in your car, drive twelve feet to another parking lot, park the car and get out. Glumly I clambered my way to a Pizza Hut and went inside, where a waitress seated me at a table with a view of the parking lot.

All around me people were eating pizzas the size of bus wheels. Directly opposite, inescapably in my line of vision, an overweight man of about thirty was lowering wedges into his mouth whole, like a sword swallower. The menu was dazzling in its variety. It went on for pages. There were so many types and sizes of pizza, so many possible combinations, that I felt quite at a loss. The waitress appeared.

'Are you ready to order?'

'I'm sorry,' I replied, 'I need a little more time.'

'Sure,' she said. 'You take your time.' She went off to somewhere out of my line of vision, counted to four and came back.

'Are you ready to order now?' she asked.

'I'm sorry,' I said, 'I really need just a little more time.'

'OK,' she said, and left. This time she may have counted as high as twenty, but when she returned I was still nowhere near understanding the many hundreds of options open to me as a Pizza Hut patron.

'You're kinda slow, arentcha?' she observed brightly.

I was embarrassed. 'I'm sorry. I'm out of touch, I've … just got out of prison.'

Her eyes widened. 'Really?'

'Yes. I murdered a waitress who rushed me.'

3 When the writer entered the restaurant he felt

   A relaxed.

   B confused.

   C disappointed.

   D relieved.

4 The man sitting opposite was

   A trying to be entertaining.

   B taking his time over his meal.

   C putting large pieces in his mouth.

   D trying to impress the writer.

5 The writer thought the menu

   A was too long.

   B offered a lot to choose from.

   C was hard to understand.

   D was made up of too many combinations.

6 The waitress

   A expected him to know what he wanted.

   B didn't know he was a foreigner.

   C got angry with him.

   D wanted to explain the menu.

7 According to the text which of the following does the writer find sad?

   A the service in America

   B the range of choice in America

   C modern towns in America

   D overweight people

**5** Find the adjective 'overweight' in the text. What does it mean? 'Over-' can be used in front of many adjectives with the meaning 'too' or 'too much'. Think of the adjective with 'over-' that you might use in the following situations:

1 To describe something you feel is too expensive

2 To describe a resort with too many people

3 To describe a country with too many people

4 To describe a parent who worries too much about their children

5 To describe someone who is too good for a job

6 To describe a library book that should have been returned

7 To describe people who have too much to do at work

8 To describe a star who you think gets too much attention

## Writing

### Organising your life at exam time

**1** Here is an article which was written to give parents and pupils advice about dealing with exam stress. Three alternative beginnings for each paragraph are given. Which one best fits the general tone of the article?

**A** *Shall I advise pupils / So what advice is there for pupils / Will you take some advice for pupils* wanting to make sure that their chances of success are not undermined by exam nerves or poor revision?

**B** *According to Childline, / Childline would like to announce that / You can bet Childline knows* young people facing exams should recognise the importance of performing well, but should remember 'that there is a life beyond revision and exams'.

**C** *We've got loads of exams, / The exam season is upon us, / Not exam time again*, with thousands of families suffering a period of stress as ambitions for getting a job, staying on at school or finding a place at university are put to the test.

**D** *To both of you, / For both pupils and parents, / With regard to parents and pupils*, Childline says that they should not be afraid to seek help when there are questions about school work, or problems with over-anxiousness that cannot be readily resolved.

**E** *On most school days for the next few weeks, / In modern times, / It's just great that* pupils are taking their different GCSE and A level papers, and Standard and Higher Grade exams.

**F** *Don't you just love Childline / Childline, the charity / A big hand for Childline* which offers confidential advice for young people, has published its own suggestions for both parents and pupils for taking as much stress as possible out of exams.

**2** The paragraphs are in jumbled order. Decide on the best order.

**3** The section giving advice to parents and pupils is missing. Write this section. Divide it into two parts: Advice for parents and Advice for pupils. You may choose to write two separate paragraphs or an introductory line for each part followed by bullet points. The Language box will help you.

**4** Decide on the best position for the new section in the article.

## Grammar

**1** All the sentences in this task are related to the grammar of comparatives and superlatives looked at in this unit in the Student's Book.

**exam task** Complete the second sentence so that it has a similar meaning to the first sentence using the word given. Do **not** change the word given. You must use between two and five words, including the word given.

EXAMPLE: I didn't think it would be so difficult.
It was ...*a lot more difficult than*.... **lot**
I expected.

1 This one is probably the easiest of the three.
This one is probably ........................... the other two.
**difficult**

2 Contacting other people is far easier than it used to be.
People can be contacted ........................... they used to be.
**more**

3 The price of bus tickets has doubled.
It now ........................... to buy a bus ticket. **twice**

4 I don't think life is better today than it was in the past.
I don't think people today live ........................... they used to.
**as**

5 The capital is much bigger than any other city in the country.
The capital is ........................... city in the country. **by**

6 Getting a passport is much quicker in my country.
It doesn't take ........................... a passport in my country.
**as**

7 There's no difference in the way we live.
Their way of life is ........................... ours. **just**

8 It used to be less expensive to eat out.
You can't eat out ........................... you used to. **as**

**2** **exam task** Here is an extract from an interview with Geri Halliwell – ex-member of the pop group the Spice Girls. Read the text below, and think of the word which best fits each space. Use only **one** word in each space.

Last night I **(1)** ..... *It's a Wonderful Life*, with James Stewart. It's one of my favourite movies. He thinks life is **(2)** ..... bad that he wishes he **(3)** ..... never been born. And then the angel shows him how the world **(4)** ..... have been if he hadn't been born and he realises **(5)** ..... many people he has touched in his life. And when you look at life **(6)** ..... that you think: 'Well actually, there is so **(7)** ..... more out there that is positive and far **(8)** ..... satisfying than your outward body image.' It's how you do it, more **(9)** ..... what you are. That's what **(10)** ..... you who you are.

## Vocabulary

### 'Life' and related words

**1** Look at the sentences below. Complete each example with one of the following words:

> life    lifetime    live
> living    lifestyle    lives

1 In my ............................ I hope to see things get better.

2 The way of ............................ on the islands is very traditional.

3 European countries enjoy a high standard of ............................ .

4 Newspapers should not interfere with people's private ............................ .

5 Her ............................ changed dramatically after she won the money.

6 In real ............................ he is a very different character to the one in the film.

7 I've never been to a ............................ concert.

8 How does he earn his ............................ ?

9 Young people today do not have a healthy ............................ .

10 I couldn't afford to study there: the cost of ............................ is so high.

**2** **exam task** Use the word given in capitals at the end of each line to form a word that fits in the space in the same line. There is an example at the beginning **(0)**.

### LAS VEGAS

| | |
|---|---|
| Like most other American cities, | |
| Las Vegas has its share of **(0)** ...~~poverty~~.. , drugs, | **POOR** |
| **(1)** ..... and homeless people. While the city's | **VIOLENT** |
| **(2)** ..... has boomed recently,  the poverty rate has soared | **ECONOMIC** |
| by 17 percent. Twelve out of every 1,000 people have | |
| been victims of violent **(3)** ..... . Of the nation's 75 largest | **CRIMINAL** |
| counties, Clark County ranks 72nd in **(4)** ..... of college | **PERCENT** |
| **(5)** ..... . | **GRADUATE** |

| | |
|---|---|
| Still, for thousands of new **(6)** ..... the promise of Las Vegas | **RESIDE** |
| is just too good to pass up. Many wage a **(7)** ..... battle to | **DAY** |
| separate their lives from the casinos. The result is the **(8)** ..... | **EMERGE** |
| of two Las Vegases. 'We operate **(9)** ..... outside the world | **TOTAL** |
| of the casinos,' said Alan Bond, father of three and manager | |
| of a mall east of the Strip. 'We just think of them as a blob | |
| of real estate downtown that we avoid.' | |

| | |
|---|---|
| Other families, however, **(10)** ..... at Las Vegas's explosive | **ALARM** |
| **(11)** ..... , are elbowing their way out of the valley. 'It's | **GROW** |
| so **(12)** ..... ,' said Nancy Rawlings Johnson, who was born | **CROWD** |
| and raised in Las Vegas. 'It's **(13)** ..... but I just don't feel | **DEPRESS** |
| **(14)** ..... here any more.' | **SAFETY** |

# Preparation for speaking

**1** Here are two photographs which show different aspects of two very different ways of life.

In Part 2 of the Speaking paper you will be asked to **compare and contrast** two photographs. Look at the questions in the box for ideas. Make notes on the points you can compare and contrast between these two photographs.

**2** As well as being asked to compare and contrast the photographs in a general way you will also be asked to comment on or speculate about an aspect of the photographs. Note down answers to these questions:

- What different types of problems may these people face in their lives?
- What kind of work do you think each person might do and who might they work for?
- Which way of life would you prefer and why?

**3** Bring your notes to class and work with another student. Take it in turns to ask each other to compare and contrast the photos and comment on them in **one** of the ways mentioned in **2**.

Where was each photo taken?
How do the people usually spend their day?
How are they dressed?
Why was each photo taken?
Who are the other people in the photo?

# Exam focus  Paper 3 Use of English

## Part 4  Error correction

In the Error-correction task you have to decide whether each *line* of a text contains a word which should not be there. Be careful, however, to read each line as part of a whole sentence. You are not really reading for meaning in this task but reading to spot words which are *not grammatically possible or correct in context.*

As you complete the exam task below, pause after each sentence and ask yourself the following questions:
- Does it contain words which cannot be used together in English?
- Are there any words which are used incorrectly?
- Is every word correct in the context of the text?

**1** **exam task** Read the text below and look carefully at each line. Some of the lines are correct, and some have a word which should not be there. If a line is correct, put a tick (✓) next to it. If a line has a word which should not be there, write the word at the end of the line. There are two examples at the beginning (**0** and **00**).

**2** Look back at the lines which contain a word which should not be there in **1**. Write the line number next to the area of grammar the error is linked to.

> article/determiner   relative clause   comparative
> use of preposition   linking word   time adverb
> active/passive verb   auxiliary verb   modal verb

These are among the most common areas of grammar tested in this task.

---

### THE VILLAGE

| 0 | Most people in my country have only lived in cities for the past | ✓ |
|---|---|---|
| 00 | thirty years. Before that they have lived in villages or small towns | *have* |
| 1 | by the sea or in the mountains. This is why it is not unusual to | |
| 2 | hear even young children who they have lived in cities all their lives | |
| 3 | talking about 'their village'. What they mean is the place where | |
| 4 | their parents were grew up or previous generations of their family | |
| 5 | lived.  Even today although 'the village' is an important part of the | |
| 6 | lives of the majority of people who now make their living in cities. | |
| 7 | Most families still have yet a house in a village somewhere around | |
| 8 | the country and they return at there in the summer or during other | |
| 9 | holidays to help with the family land or just to spend time with | |
| 10 | friends and relatives. There is a wonderful sense of community and | |
| 11 | a shared past in each these villages which is so different from the | |
| 12 | cities in where most of us live. If these villages can survive, I am | |
| 13 | sure people will find it more easier to spend time in them in the future. | |
| 14 | People who have made money in the cities will start to can invest | |
| 15 | in their old family homes and help to maintain this lovely aspect of | |
|  | family life in my country. | |

# 14 Planet matters

## Reading

**1** Look at the headline for this article. What might have happened to this boy? Jot down some ideas, then read the article to check your predictions.

---

### Boy survives six days on icy mountain

A 14-year-old snowboarder missing for six days and feared dead was found alive on a Californian mountainside after surviving blizzards and freezing temperatures. 'Someone upstairs was looking out for him,' said Art Fortini.  **0** H

**1** [ ] The spot is at 1,700 metres in the Mountain High ski area about 100 kilometres northeast of Los Angeles.

He was airlifted to a nearby hospital where doctors reported he was in a stable condition although dehydrated. **2** [ ] His parents were flown in to be reunited with the boy who had been feared dead. Jeff was 'hungry, tired and cold' but otherwise appeared in good shape, a Los Angeles County Sheriff's Department spokesman said.

Jeff disappeared on the afternoon of February 7 while snowboarding with his uncle. On Friday afternoon, Mr Fortini and Randy Katai found footprints in the snow and followed them to find the youth sitting by a stream. **3** [ ] 'He's been through an ordeal. He took some kind of fall.'

Mr Fortini said that although Jeff had no food, he could at least drink water from the stream. **4** [ ] Mr Katai said the young snowboarder appeared to have gone out of bounds on the ski slope and got lost. **5** [ ]

At the height of the search 120 rescuers, two helicopters and two rescue dogs combed the mountain looking for him. The search was hampered by heavy snow and winds up to 125 km/h.

Sheriff's deputy Benita Nichols said Jeff was 'alive and alert, although exhausted' when he was found 'in the area where they have been searching for him for the last few days.' **6** [ ]

---

**2** **exam task** Seven sentences have been removed from the article. Choose from the sentences **A–H** the one which fits each gap (**1–6**). There is an extra sentence which you do not need to use. There is an example at the beginning (**0**).

**A** He also had some frostbite and his body temperature had fallen to about 34 degrees Celsius.

**B** She said there was no word on how he had survived the ordeal.

**C** Jeff Thornton had survived for six days with no food, in freezing night temperatures and daytime blizzards in a place near Bear Gulch.

**D** 'I yelled his name and he turned round and looked at me and I knew he was alive,' Mr Katai said.

**E** Bears and wolves are sometimes seen in the area.

**F** It was a very steep, rugged area and he had been unable to climb back up to the ski area.

**G** But 'how he survived the storms ... I have no answer.'

**H** Mr Fortini is one of two Sierra Madre Search and Rescue team members who found the missing boy.

---

**3** Match these words from the article to their meaning:

| Word | | Meaning in the article |
|---|---|---|
| 1 | a blizzard | **a** without enough water in your body |
| 2 | to airlift | **b** a small river |
| 3 | dehydrated | **c** damage to your fingers, toes, etc. caused by extreme cold |
| 4 | frostbite | **d** rising sharply |
| 5 | snowboarding | **e** rocky and rough |
| 6 | a stream | **f** a very bad snow storm with strong winds |
| 7 | steep | **g** extremely tired |
| 8 | rugged | **h** a very difficult experience |
| 9 | an ordeal | **i** to carry somebody or something out of a place by air |
| 10 | exhausted | **j** a sport involving travelling through snow on a board |

**4** What would you have done if you had been Jeff? Complete these sentences.
Be careful to choose the right conditional construction in each case.

1 If I had got lost while snowboarding I ...........................................................................................................

2 If I had had no food for six days I ...........................................................................................................

3 If I had found a stream, I ...........................................................................................................

4 If I had been struck by snow storms and freezing temperatures I ...........................................................

5 When I heard my rescuers' voices I ...........................................................................................................

6 If I had the opportunity to go snowboarding again I ...........................................................................................................

7 If I went snowboarding in a dangerous place I ...........................................................................................................

**5** Imagine you are Jeff after the rescue. Write a letter to a friend explaining
what happened to you, how you survived and were rescued, and how you
feel about your ordeal.

## Writing

**Formats in articles and reports**

**1** This article has no paragraphs and some incorrect punctuation.
Read it through, and mark where the paragraphs should begin
and end, and correct the punctuation and related mistakes.

# Lost men with cash to burn survive

Five snowmobilers who burned their cash, credit cards and wallets to stay warm after they were forced to spend a night near a freezing lake. Were found in good condition. The men, who had been snowmobiling together for five years, apparently became stuck in snow at Moon Lake, near Mount Bachelor, in the northwestern state of Oregon. On Saturday afternoon and had not returned by dark. Friends notified the authorities. Who found nothing that night. The men – John Winters, 26, Kenny Fordice, 37, Kip Templeton, 36, Joe Thurey, 37, and Kent Maitland, 30, all from around state capital Portland. Tried to walk to safety on Saturday night but realised they would have to spend the night outdoors. Although regular snowmobilers, the men were not prepared for an extended stay in the snow. Two were not wearing winter boots. And the group had no snow shovel nor ground covering. Rescue coordinator Wayne Inman said the men still managed to build a make-shift shelter. And sacrificed their possessions in the fire. 'It was pretty ingenious and it probably saved their lives,' he said. Several hundred people searched for the men on Sunday. The men stumbled on another group of snowmobilers. With a cell phone, in the afternoon. 'If we hadn't made it out today, we thought we would die.' Mr Templeton said.

**2** Here is a short report. Its layout could be improved in various ways: by using headings, bullets points and/or numbering, and by putting the information in a different order. Rewrite the report to improve these features.

## Can rhinos survive?

Rhino horn is used to make ornaments and medicines. It has been used for these purposes for centuries. Nowadays, however, the decrease in rhino numbers and the increase in the illegal export of rhino horn threaten to wipe out the African continent's rhino population. This report gives the results of a survey into current rhino populations and makes recommendations about how to protect them.

The survey was carried out by Traffic, a wildlife trade monitoring programme. It found that outside southern Africa only 192 white rhino and 427 black rhino remained in the world. More than 22,000 rhino have been killed since 1970 to meet market demands. Poaching was found to be taking place in the Democratic Republic of Congo, and in Kenya and Tanzania, with Sudan being the major exporter of rhino horn.

Reasons why the trade continues include the very high price fetched by rhino horn: more than $1,000 per kilogram, and the fact that customs officers are easy targets for bribery.

Traffic recommends the introduction of sniffer dogs into customs services. Education of the public to encourage them not to buy products made from rhino horn is also very important.

## Grammar

**1**  For questions **1–10**, read the text below and decide which answer **A, B, C** or **D** best fits each space. There is an example at the beginning **(0)**.

### Punches free man from jaws of crocodile

A 35-year-old man told yesterday how he **(0)** ..C.. punched a crocodile to free himself from its jaws **(1)** ..... an attack in north Queensland, Australia.

Police said Ron Bakx suffered cuts to his head, arm, back and right shoulder after **(2)** ..... bitten by the two-metre crocodile off a beach at Yorkeys Knob near Cairns, Northern Australia, on Friday evening.

He was at a beach party when he decided to take a swim to cool **(3)** ..... and was attacked in waist deep water. 'I dived in and it attacked me,' Mr Bakx told the *Sunday Telegraph*. 'I didn't think I **(4)** ..... be here today. It tried to **(5)** ..... me under in a death roll. He was really going for it. It had half my head and shoulder. I was really freaking out.'

Mr Bakx said his friends watched from the beach as he **(6)** ..... and punched the animal, which **(7)** ..... let him go. 'I got free and **(8)** ..... backwards at a hundred miles an hour,' he said.

He was **(9)** ..... to Cairns Base Hospital, where he was **(10)** ..... with painkillers.

| 0 | **A** occasionally | **B** hardly | **C** repeatedly | **D** again |
|---|---|---|---|---|
| 1 | **A** between | **B** through | **C** while | **D** during |
| 2 | **A** been | **B** be | **C** was | **D** being |
| 3 | **A** out | **B** off | **C** away | **D** up |
| 4 | **A** will | **B** 'd | **C** am | **D** may |
| 5 | **A** push | **B** drag | **C** tear | **D** bite |
| 6 | **A** cried | **B** kicked | **C** attacked | **D** opposed |
| 7 | **A** lastly | **B** hopefully | **C** definitely | **D** eventually |
| 8 | **A** rushed | **B** went | **C** fell | **D** ran |
| 9 | **A** asked | **B** taken | **C** pushed | **D** removed |
| 10 | **A** treated | **B** cured | **C** healed | **D** doctored |

**2** Look at these cartoons. Write sentences in reply to the questions. Be ready to talk about them in class.

### Speculating about past events

What would you have done in this situation as

- Ron Bakx?
- one of his friends?
- the crocodile?

Write five sentences using the third conditional tense to answer these questions.

### Speculating about unlikely future events

What would you do if you saw these things?

Write five sentences, using the second conditional tense to answer this question.

*Some possible future date*

# Vocabulary

**1** **exam task** Read the text below. Use the word given in capitals at the end of each line to form a word that fits in the space in the same line. There is an example at the beginning (0).

## Eco-tourism

Eco-tourism is a **(0)** *fashionable* label for travel concerned with the | **FASHION**
environment. Such holidays are by no means new, but they are more
popular than ever before. They offer an opportunity to visit **(1)** ..... | **RELATIVE**
undisturbed **(2)** ..... areas to view and study the flora and fauna, | **NATURE**
often combined with **(3)** ..... the local indigenous culture. | **UNDERSTAND**

Many people see them not only as a way of contributing but also
as a means of putting adventure, **(4)** ..... and stimulation back into travel. | **DISCOVER**
They feel they are part of the **(5)** ..... , not part of the problem. | **SOLVE**

Earthwatch was one of the pioneer eco-tourism companies. It let **(6)** ..... | **ADVENTURE**
travellers sign on for whale-watching and bird-banding **(7)** ..... expeditions. | **SCIENCE**
'Many people,' says Andrew Mitchell, the deputy **(8)** ..... 'long to use their | **DIRECT**
holiday time in a more useful way, and scientists involved in crucial field
research need committed, interested **(9)** ..... . The work is sometimes the | **ASSIST**
final chance to preserve some of our **(10)** ..... environmental and cultural | **VANISH**
heritage for future generations.'

**2** Use prefixes and suffixes to make a list of as many words as you can from these words:

> fashion    science    use

**3** Find a picture of objects or scenes related to any aspect of the environment. Think about how to describe it, then in your next lesson, play 'Describe and Draw'. Working with a partner, tell him or her what is in your picture. Your partner must draw (however unartistically!) what you describe **without** looking at your original picture. At the end compare the original and the drawing.

# Preparation for speaking

All of these animals are endangered and could face extinction.

Think about your answers to these questions and be ready to discuss them in class:

- Should these animals be protected by being put in zoos?
- Should people be punished for killing them?
- Does it matter if they become extinct? Why?

Black rhino

Panda

Snow leopard

Condor

Grey whale

Indian elephant

# Exam focus  Paper 5 Speaking

## Helping yourself

**1** In Section C of Units 5, 10 and 14 of the Student's Book you have seen what the different parts of the Speaking paper are like, and what you are required to do. Read these sections of the Student's Book again (pages 66, 130 and 182) and complete this table.

| Part | Who speaks and who to? | What kind of information is discussed? | What kind of task do you need to carry out? | How long does this part last? |
|------|------------------------|----------------------------------------|---------------------------------------------|-------------------------------|
| 1 |  |  |  |  |
| 2 |  |  |  |  |
| 3 |  |  |  |  |
| 4 |  |  |  |  |

**2** Which part would you find easiest and which most difficult? Write notes explaining why.

**3** Which of these is the biggest/ smallest challenge for you for Paper 5? Write notes explaining why.
- Organising and linking your ideas and words well
- Good pronunciation (sounds, stress, intonation)
- Using grammar and vocabulary accurately and widely
- Carrying out the task requirements
- Successful interaction

**4** Here are some suggestions for how to improve your speaking skills outside class. Which ones would you find useful? Tick them.

1 Practising reading aloud short passages in English
2 Holding conversations with yourself in English, recording them and listening to them
3 Chatting with friends and/or family in English
4 Doing extra grammar exercises
5 Borrowing books on vocabulary from a library
6 Talking with tourists
7 Holding mock exam interviews with small groups of friends
8 Identifying sounds that are a problem for you, then practising saying them out loud by yourself
9 Visiting English language learning sites on the Internet
10 Any other ideas: ........................................................

**5** Prepare a four-minute talk for the class on 'What I need to do to prepare myself for FCE Paper 5 and why'. You could give the talk in pairs or groups, or even to the whole class.

# Dealing with the FCE exam

## Content, marking and exam tips

### An overview of the FCE exam

The FCE exam consists of five papers, as follows:

| Paper | Focus | No. of questions | Timing |
|---|---|---|---|
| Paper 1 | Reading | 35 | 1 hour 15 minutes |
| Paper 2 | Writing | 2 pieces of writing | 1 hour 30 minutes |
| Paper 3 | Use of English | 65 | 1 hour 15 minutes |
| Paper 4 | Listening | 30 | 40 minutes (approx.) |
| Paper 5 | Speaking | 4 parts | 14 minutes (approx.) |

### Paper 1 Reading

#### Content

| Part | Task type and focus | No. of questions |
|---|---|---|
| 1 | Multiple matching (understanding main points) | 6 or 7 |
| 2 | Multiple choice (understanding detail) | 7 or 8 |
| 3 | Gapped text (understanding text structure) | 6 or 7 |
| 4 | Multiple matching (understanding specific information) | 13–15 |

#### Marking

Questions 1–20 (Parts 1–3) carry two marks each, and questions 21–35 (Part 4) carry one mark each.

#### Tips

**Part 1 Multiple matching**

- Look at the title or headline, then quickly read through the first few paragraphs to get a general idea of what the text is about. Next read the headings or summary sentences.
- Then, as you read each paragraph carefully, underline four or five words which together give the main idea of what the paragraph is about.
- Read each paragraph several times and try to match the paragraph to one of the headings or summary sentences.
- Keep an open mind and be prepared to change your answers as you read further into the text.

**Part 2 Multiple choice**

- Quickly read through the first few paragraphs of the text to get an idea of what the text is about. Then read the whole text carefully.
- When answering the questions first decide which part of the text a question relates to. Remember that some questions relate to the whole text.
- Before deciding which option (A, B, C or D) is correct, find reasons in the text to eliminate the three other options.
- When you are asked questions like 'What does *it* in line xx refer to?' read the sentence substituting 'it' with the possible answers. By doing this, you can check which answer makes sense both in the sentence and the paragraph as a whole.
- When answering questions about the whole text, think about the layout, the type of information the text contains and its style.

## Part 3 Gapped text

- First predict from the title or headline what the text might be about and quickly read through the text to confirm this.
- Read the paragraphs or sentences that go in the gaps and identify what the topic of each one is. Use this information to work out how they might logically fit into the sequence of the text.
- Think about what the articles, pronouns, conjunctions and time expressions in the paragraphs or sentences might refer to.
- Closely read the sentences before and after each gap, and work out what function the missing sentence or paragraph must have.
- Make your decisions, not necessarily in order. After filling most of the gaps you may be able to work by a process of elimination.
- Finally, when you have made all your decisions, read through your completed text to make sure it makes sense.

## Part 4 Multiple matching

- Quickly familiarise yourself with the main text, the title and headings and how the text is divided up. Then read the questions.
- Read the text to locate information rather than to understand it in detail. Look at each question and then scan the text to locate where the information might be found.
- When you think you have located the correct information, decide whether the word or phrase you have located in the text is an accurate paraphrase of the word or phrase in the question.
- Be prepared to change your first answers, because you may change your mind when you read the text further in search of another piece of information.
- Mark the places in the text where you locate answers so that you can quickly check through at the end.

# Paper 2 Writing

## Content

| Part | Task type and focus | No. of questions |
|------|---------------------|------------------|
| 1 | Writing a formal or informal transactional letter | One letter (120–180 words) |
| 2 | Writing one task from the following:<br>● an article<br>● an informal/non-transactional letter<br>● a report<br>● a discursive composition<br>● a descriptive / narrative composition / short story<br>● one of the above on a background reading text | One piece of writing (120–180 words) |

## Marking

UCLES marks the writing tasks on a scale of 1–5 in which band 3 is considered satisfactory. The assessors bear in mind the following criteria when they mark:

- content
- organisation and cohesion
- range and accuracy of structures and vocabulary
- register and format
- effect on target reader

They also make use of task-specific mark schemes. Each question carries equal marks.

## Tips

### Part 1 Transactional letters

- Read all the information included in the question very carefully and underline all the points you are told to include.
- Before writing, decide:
  - your reason for writing;
  - who you are writing to and how this will affect your style of writing;
  - what result you hope the letter will achieve.
- Make a draft or outline of the letter to check that you have included all the points and grouped or organised them in a logical way.
- Read your letter through when it is written and think about the person who is going to receive it and whether it would have the right effect.

**Part 2 Article, discursive composition, letter, report, set book questions**

- Choose a question where you have a good idea of the style and format the piece of writing requires.
- Answer the question. Do not just write in a general way or make something you have written before try to fit the question.
- Follow this procedure for writing: brainstorm your ideas on paper; organise and link your ideas; write a first draft; edit your first draft; write your final draft.
- Go into the exam with a clear idea of the kinds of writing mistakes you often make, then when you are editing your work, keep a special look-out for these kinds of mistakes.

---

# Paper 3 Use of English

## Content

| Part | Task type and focus | No. of questions |
|------|---------------------|------------------|
| 1 | Multiple-choice cloze (an emphasis on vocabulary) | 15 |
| 2 | Open cloze (grammar and vocabulary) | 15 |
| 3 | 'Key' word-transformation (grammar and vocabulary) | 10 |
| 4 | Error correction (an emphasis on grammar) | 15 |
| 5 | Word formation (vocabulary) | 15 |

## Marking

Questions 1–30 and 41–65 (Parts 1, 2, 4 and 5) carry one mark, and questions 31–40 (Part 3) carry two marks each.

## Tips

### Part 1 Multiple-choice cloze

- Read the text through first to get a good idea of what it is about.
- Think about the meaning of the missing word.
- Look at the words before and after the gap and think about why some of the options will not fit in the gap. You will often have to think about the grammar of these words.
- Try to eliminate three of the options before choosing the correct one.
- Read the whole text through after you have written your answers to make sure your answers make sense.

### Part 2 Open cloze

- Look at the title and read the text through to get a good idea of what it is about.
- Think about what part of speech (verb, preposition, conjunction, etc.) each missing word could be.
- Think about different words that could fit in the gap and then choose the one that fits best in the context of the sentence and the text as a whole.
- When you have filled all the gaps, read the text through to make sure everything makes sense.

### Part 3 'Key' word-transformation

- Think about the first sentence and different ways of expressing the same idea.
- Remember your answer will include at least *two but not more than five* words.
- Think about what grammar or vocabulary point is being tested, e.g. changing an active form to a passive form and all the changes you will have to make in completing the second sentence.
- Using the 'key' word will involve you in making more than one change to the original sentence, e.g. with the 'key' word '*instead*', '*rather than go*' becomes '*instead of going*'.

## Part 4 Error correction

- Read the whole text through first.
- Read each *sentence* carefully before deciding whether there is a mistake in the *line*.
- Read as if you are looking for mistakes. Ask yourself questions like: 'Do we need an article or preposition, etc. here?' 'Should this verb be active or passive?'
- Remember that some things may look grammatically correct, but they may not be correct in the context.
- Remember you are only looking for words which *must* be removed because they make the sentence ungrammatical.

## Part 5 Word formation

- Read through the whole text first to find out what it is about.
- First decide what part of speech is needed in the gap.
- When you have decided what type of word is needed, e.g. noun or verb, decide whether you have to add a grammatical ending, e.g. make it plural or add -*ing*.
- Also think about the meaning of the text and whether you have to add a prefix, e.g. make a positive form negative by adding a prefix.
- Think carefully about spelling and whether the spelling of the word you are forming varies from the word you are given.

# Paper 4 Listening

## Content

| Part | Task type and focus | No. of questions |
|------|---------------------|------------------|
| 1 | Multiple choice (understanding gist, main points, detail, function, location, roles and relationships mood, attitude, intention, feeling or opinion) | 8 |
| 2 | Note taking or Blank filling (understanding gist, main points, detail or specific information, or deducing meaning) | 10 |
| 3 | Multiple matching (as for Part 1) | 5 |
| 4 | Multiple choice or Selection (as for Part 2) | 7 |

## Marking

Each of the 30 questions carries one mark.

## Tips

### Part 1 Multiple choice

- You may have to pay attention to stress and intonation, the speed at which the speakers speak and/or their sex, role, age and manner (hesitation, etc.). Listen for information which helps you to eliminate wrong options as well as identify correct ones.

### Part 2 Note taking or Blank filling

- Questions in both types of task follow the same sequence as the information heard on the recording.
- You will need to write between one and three words for each answer. Do not write longer answers.
- You will not lose a mark for incorrect spelling if it is clear what word you intended to write, except where a word is spelt out for you on the recording.
- In the blank-filling task your answers have to be grammatically correct within the sentence, so check your answers for this at the end of the recording.
- Try to write down an answer to all the questions as you listen to the recording the first time, and then confirm whether your answer is right or needs changing as you listen the second time.

### Part 3 Multiple matching

- Read the questions through carefully beforehand in the time you are given before listening. Think about the focus of the question. For example, are you listening to decide on the speaker, or the place, etc.?
- Don't try to understand every word or every part of the listening text. Concentrate on listening for ideas or words on the recording that relate to key words in the questions.
- Try to write down the answers when you hear the recording the first time and then confirm or change them the second time you hear the recording.

### Part 4 Multiple choice or Selection

- Use the time you are given before the recording starts to read through the questions and think about the options. Predict, for example, what you might hear on the recording if something is true or what you might hear if it is false.
- The information is given on the recording in the same order as the questions, so make sure you focus on the right question at the right time.
- Try to note down the answers the first time you hear the recording and then confirm or change them the second time you listen.

## Paper 5 Speaking

## Content

You will take this paper with another candidate, or perhaps in a group of three candidates. You will be examined by an interlocutor who gives you all the instructions and materials, and by an assessor who listens to your performance.

| Part | Task type and focus | Timing |
|------|---------------------|--------|
| 1 | Interview: Interlocutor interviews each candidate (responding to questions and expanding on responses) | 3 minutes |
| 2 | Individual long turn: Each candidate carries out an individual task in which they compare and contrast photographs giving information and expressing opinions through comparing and contrasting | 4 minutes |
| 3 | Collaborative task: candidates talk with one another (turn-taking and negotiating, exchanging information and opinions, expressing and justifying opinions, agreeing and/or disagreeing, suggesting, speculating) | 3 minutes |
| 4 | Discussion: candidates talk with one another and the interlocutor (responding appropriately, developing topics, exchanging information and opinions, expressing and justifying opinions, agreeing and/or disagreeing) | 4 minutes |

## Marking

You are assessed on your performance throughout the paper. The examiners mark according to the following criteria:

- grammar and vocabulary
- discourse management
- pronunciation
- interactive communication

## Tips

### Part 1 Interview

- This part of the paper is your opportunity to give information about yourself.
- Answer the questions fully and naturally. Remember to expand on short answers.
- Respond to your partner's answers with interest.
- Relax!

### Part 2 Individual long turn

- Listen carefully to the interlocutor's instructions. He or she will ask you to **compare and contrast** two photographs **and** to speculate or give an opinion about one aspect of them.
- Think about using language that will allow you to move comfortably from one photograph to the other and back again. This language has been highlighted for you in the Speaking sections of the Student's Book.
- Make meaningful comparisons between the pictures that relate to the interlocutor's question.
- You have a minute. If you dry up, simply talk about another aspect of the pictures.

### Part 3 Collaborative task

- Listen carefully to the instructions the interlocutor gives, and make sure you follow them. If you don't understand, ask for further explanation. Note that it is most unlikely that you will need to describe the pictures. Follow the instructions.
- Relax!
- Take part in the discussion fully and helpfully. Try neither to dominate your partner nor to be dominated. Give your opinion, get your partner's opinion, and talk about them together.
- Don't overuse expressions you have learnt, as you will make your discussion sound unnatural if you do.
- If you can't remember or don't know any language, don't worry. Find another way of saying the same thing.
- Don't feel you have to talk about everything in the pictures. Just try to complete the task the interlocutor sets.

### Part 4 Discussion

- Listen carefully to the interlocutor's questions and make sure your answers are relevant. Ask for explanation if you don't understand.
- Listen carefully to your partner's answers as you may think of things you wish to add.
- Expand on your answers: give reasons, examples, etc. and relate the questions to your own experience.

*You might like to visit the UCLES website* **http://www.cambridge-efl.org** *if you wish to see further information from the FCE Handbook, sample FCE papers or FCE examiners' reports.*